For Jo, Thomas & Theo

© Paul Gaskell 2020

The photographic images, diagrams and/or text portions of this book or parts thereof may not be reproduced in any form, stored in any retrieval system, or transmitted in any form by any means—electronic, mechanical, photocopy, recording, or otherwise—without prior written permission of the publisher, except as provided by United States of America and/or international copyright law. For permission requests, write to the publisher, at "Attention: Permissions Coordinator," at the address below:

Paul Gaskell

paul@fishingdiscoveries.com

Website: fishingdiscoveries.com

Don't Miss Your Video Content & Bonuses

Includes **72-minute video** feature plus bonus chapters to the book and more

Access it all online for free by typing the link or
↓ scanning the QR code below ↓

fishingdiscoveries.com/bfs-book-accompanying-video-registration

Preface

Fishing is about experiences and often the friendships it leads to. In recent years Bait Finesse System (BFS) fishing - a term first used by Shimano and now widely used to describe ultralight baitcasting - has given me a rich abundance of experiences and led to many new friends around the world. At the same time, particularly during COVID lockdown situations, it has also opened-up new and surprising adventures right on my doorstep. This book was created to share the BFS experience, make more connections with the wider bait finesse community and inspire your own adventures with ultralight baitcasting gear. I am delighted to say the lure of the round-profile reel finally let me tempt my partner in crime at Fishing Discoveries (John Pearson) into the world of BFS, so I am hopeful that our community will grow over time.

Part scrapbook/informal photo-album, part storybook and part "arty-farty" photography portfolio this book aims to tell BFS stories from the USA, Japan, UK, Malaysia, Italy, Singapore and beyond. I hope you'll find familiar experiences that represent your fishing and, more importantly, that you might also see something new that makes you go "wow".

Paul

Learning BFS one backlash at a time..

Contents

Introduction	7
Perch At the End of the Path	8
Mountain Stream Adventures in the Japanese homeland of BFS with "Tsurinan-Desu"	17
Bait finesse Reel Tour	26
Bass & More with Chris "Anorak SZN"	40
BFS with Noodles on the Side	47
Snakeheads, Kayaks, Power BFS & the Multispecies Angling Experience with Jimmy Ly	61
Pike Between the Rain Clouds	73

Malaysian Fish & Fishing with Christopher Lee Lian Li	74
Brook Trout, Trout, Panfish & Bass with Hobie-Wan Kenobi	78
Secret Creek	85
Building a Bait Finesse Empire with Amir Azzabi	90
Lockdown Perch	94
Italian Bait Finesse with Tsurikichi Nikke	96
April Fools' Trout	98
Needham's Specialist Tackle	104
God is in the Detail	108
Alan Ang: Fishing & Conservation Ambassador - Creator of the Bait Finesse Style Fishing Facebook Group	114
Rod Tour	118
John Pearson: Bait Finesse Convert Tackles the "Why Not Just Use a Spinning Reel?" Question	126
Peacock Bass in Singapore with Kevin Mai	130
Farewell Fishing Trip with Duncan...	134
Lure Tour	140
Closing Message & Profound Thanks	146

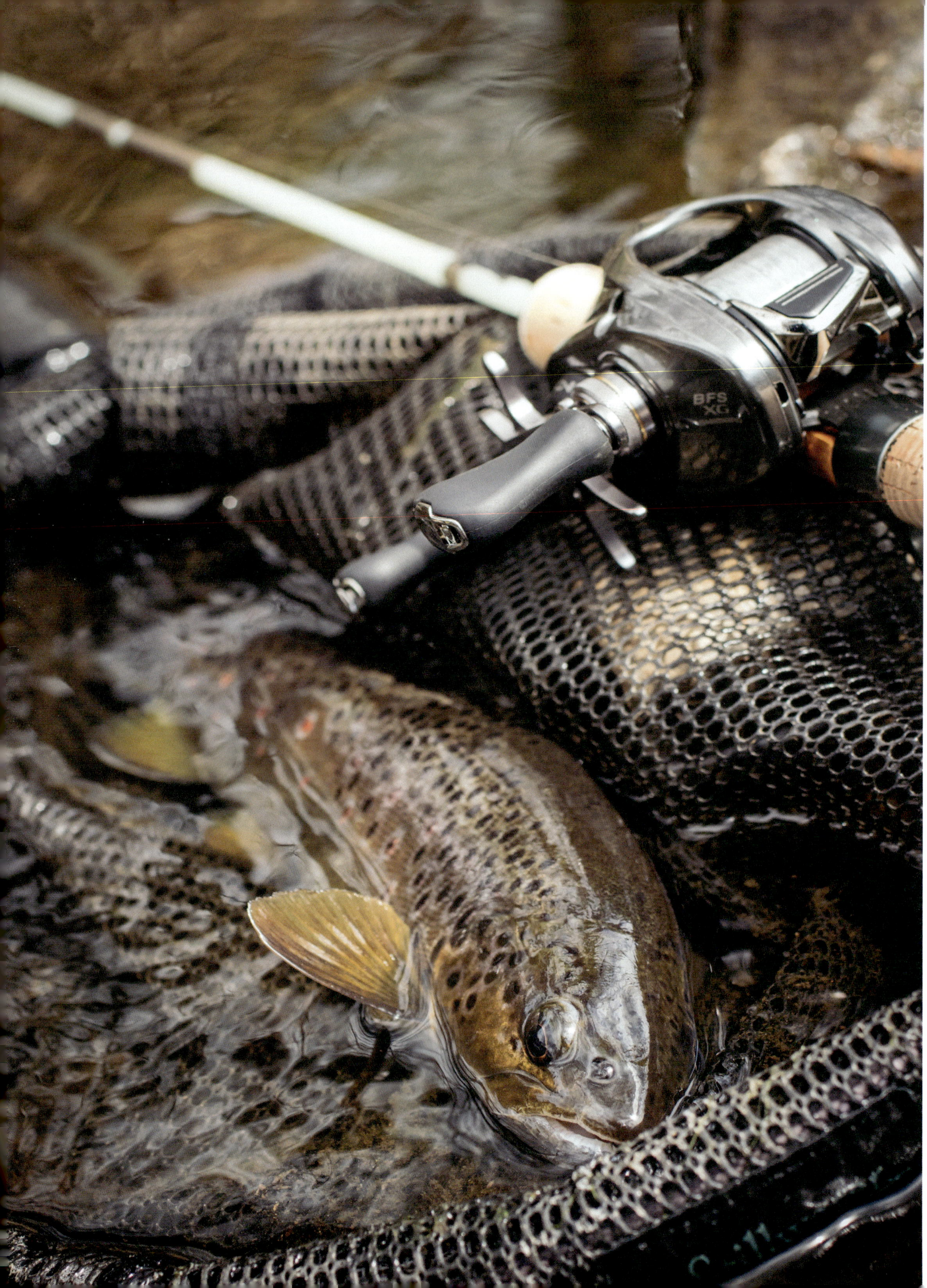
BFS
XG

INTRODUCTION

Why Create This Book?

In many ways the driver for the making this book is to answer a simple question:

"Why not just use a spinning rod and reel?"

Although there are some equally simple, practical and true replies (perhaps highlighting the lack of line-twist or the improved ability to influence the bait while in flight); capturing the full explanation is not so easy. For instance, part of what makes it difficult for me is that I genuinely enjoy ultralight spinning gear too (along with many other angling styles). How is it, then, I find some days all I want to do is cast an ultralight baitcasting rig?

To make a better attempt to answer that question, it seems important to capture the feeling of a BFS trip experienced by people who are happily addicted to the method. It almost never comes down to the dry, sterile statistics on paper when you're dealing with fishing.

Satisfaction arrives for many different reasons - and those reasons may have little to do with logic. With such a range of experiences to communicate, perhaps it is best not to rely on only one method of sharing. That's why you'll find artistic photos, informal personal snaps, trip reports, stories and profiles of BFS personalities - as well as rods, reels and lures.

Let's dive in.

Perch At the End of the Path

BFS Adventures Hiding Under Your Nose

With my local river, you never really know what you're going to get. Quite often it is a bit of a heartbreaker. You can grind away for hours with no sign of a fish; then all of a sudden something huge swipes once at your lure and then is gone (never to return).

Then again, it produces just enough days where everything works out and fishing seems like the easiest thing anyone could ever do. Just for good measure it will throw in a species that isn't supposed to be there or maybe a massive fish for such a little stream - anything to keep you guessing.

It's kind of a bitch like that - which is probably why I like it so much.

This one is about a late-summer trip where everything started out going a bit wrong. I was late getting away from work, the usual route down to the river was blocked and there seemed to be some dispute about ownership, footpaths and all kinds of things that had me thinking of a backside full of buckshot if I wasn't careful.

As a result, I had to head down an unknown path where the map said it veered close enough to the river for me to cross undisputed land to reach it. Because access looked difficult and uninviting, I hoped that by some minor miracle it might lead me into water containing fish that had escaped the attention of anglers for a long time.

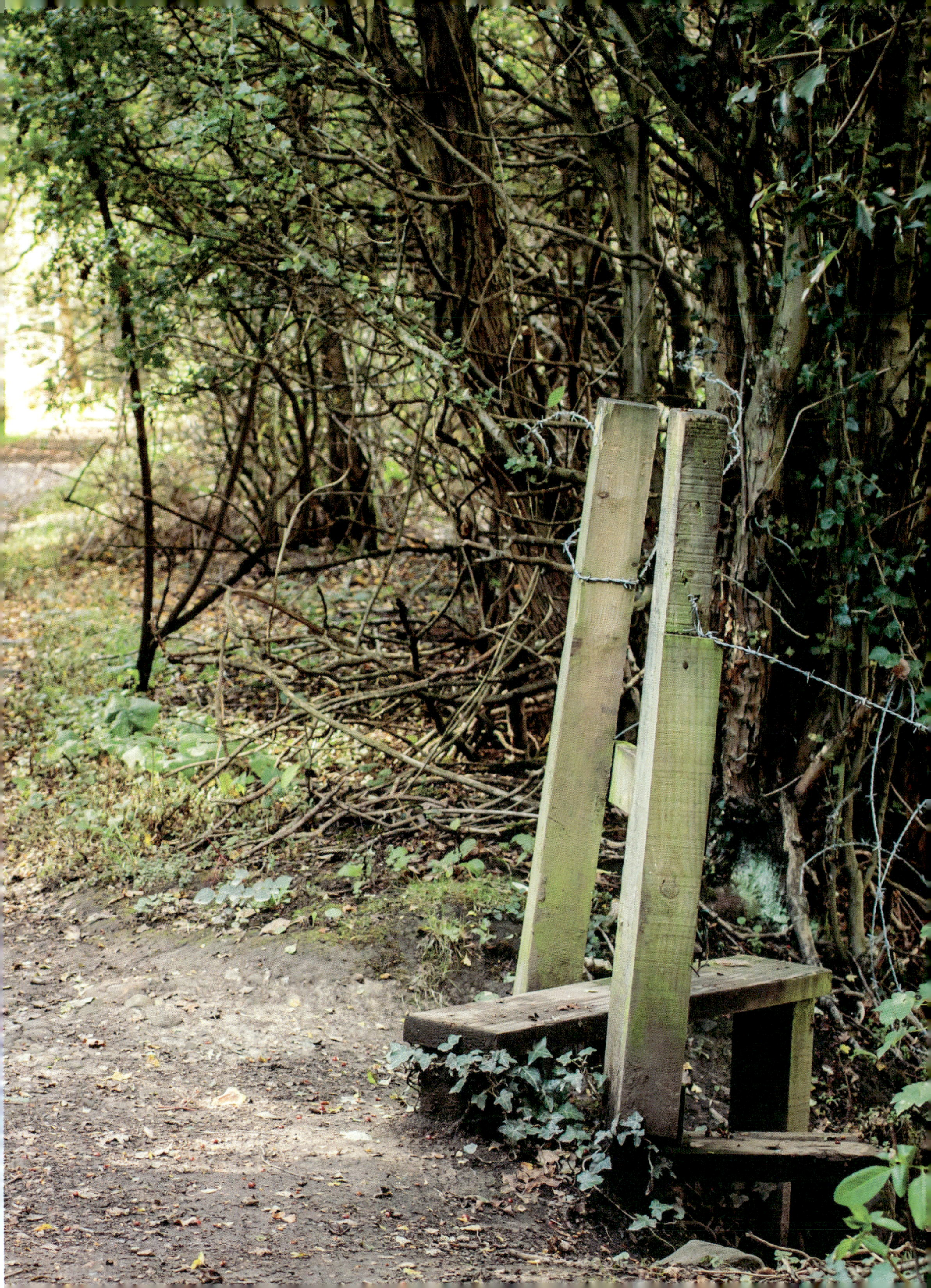

Yep,

First impressions were 100% accurate. It's an unpleasant wrestling match to get to the river. Branches poke down the back of my collar and shed a load of leaves and dirt down inside my shirt as I try to crouch low enough to break through (mind out for the unexpected eye-poke). Mud sucks at wading boots in an almost dry back-channel choked with twisted, scrubby thorn-bushes and fenced in by Himalayan balsam plants that are over head-height.

Sweating and dishevelled I break through the vegetation out onto a little gravel bar beach sloping down towards an inviting bend pool. It's necessary to brush the burst seed-pods from all that balsam out of my hair and dig some more out from down the back of my neck. No-one should be spreading that stuff around.

This looks promising though - and maybe nobody has thrashed their way through here for a while. I've rigged a 2" floating stickbait on a 3-g cheb head (hooked Texas rig style). I have no idea what fish I'll find here (or what size they might be) - but I'm hoping for perch and maybe chub too. Since that size bait has caught me good sized perch before - and it is small enough for more modest fish to grab - then perhaps this is a good hedged bet to start out with.

First cast in towards the tree roots up against the bank and the weight jangles on the gravel bottom - or was that a shy rattling bite? Surely not, the bottom must just be rough and very hard there. The next cast into the same area, though, reaches the bottom and it feels a lot softer.

Yeah, I must have missed a chance on my very first cast - dumbass (though a mildly encouraged dumbass thanks to the proof of life in this mysterious pool). Now I risk a throw straight upstream underneath those dangerous, but tempting, long, thin overhanging willow twigs just above the water. The same jangling just as the weight touches down

10

and this time, I'm not half asleep and I set the hook. A little, bristling angry "wasp" of a perch comes to the net. That's him top left on the opposite page. Looking down the camera lens I can see, although he's lying still, in his eye he's absolutely raging and sincerely wants to spike or - better - kill me at the next chance he gets.

Still, at least he's getting a good breather in the net - since I can see water pumping through his gills. When I pick him up with wetted hand (mind those thin scalpel-blade gill plates and spiky dorsal) his muscles tense up along the full length of his body. At the first touch of water he splashes my face with a wriggling tail-slap as he blasts back into the depths. I love perch. Their looks and their attitude are just extremely appealing to me. Plus, while catching tiny perch as a kid - they always fought so much harder than the small silver fish species of a similar size. I guess the distinctive feeling of a perch fight always reminds me of that pure excitement.

Some of the chunkier perch I've caught as a (so-called) grown-up would have been unimaginable to my 9-year old self. It still shocks me that those fish exist. Anyway, this first tiny perch has already made my day by rewarding the gamble of trying to fish in a completely unexplored spot. I cross the narrow channel to get around the trailing branches (it's surprisingly deep next to the bank and I nearly pitch forwards onto my face). The fat fish above comes after my first cast up into a really deep spot above the overhanging willow. It's another classic, rattling perch bite and the bend in the rod as it comes kicking and jagging towards the net lets me know that it has a deal more mass to it than the first, fizzing, angry wasp. OK, it's no monster of the deep but a perch this size on an ultralight rod is super satisfying and gives that internal mile-wide-grin feeling. This one is less angry than the first and seems quite content to just allow me to take some photos.

It scoots a short distance into the current when released and sits with its belly touching the pebbles of the gravel bar, trimming its fins and tail in the flow for several seconds before fanning steadily off down the slope and back into cover.

Turning around I wonder what might be downstream of the little gravel beach I first broke out onto. The banks are too thick with vegetation to climb out on, so casting downstream ahead of where you're walking is the only option. Because it's such a small stream at this point, I worry that there won't be very many deeper areas with enough water to appeal to larger fish. It's soon obvious that this fear is extremely stupid. I know this river just upstream is both wider and deeper in many places - and all that water flowing down from there needs to make enough space for itself here too.

I find myself standing in soft mud with the water reaching up to my chest and my waterproof camera bag is getting wet at the bottom. It's still getting deeper and the mystery of where all that water flowing from upstream fits is easily solved. Like the pool upstream, the flow is flat and fairly slow outside of the short gravel riffle section. The slowness has allowed soft silt to deposit and there's no telling how deep I would sink with one more step downstream.

Back-tracking to the gravel mini-beach and then continuing to fish upstream is the only option.

The lull in hook-ups is also a good reminder of how fortunate the previous fish captures were. Plain old failure is a helpful reminder to be grateful for what I've caught - as is the late summer/early autumn sunshine which appears in patches between the overhanging tree canopy and metres-tall , sickly sweet-smelling balsam growth. It is good to be alive.

In the late afternoon the golden glow of the sun is absolutely stunning.

Being ready for the slight drop-off next to the bank in the faster water just off the point of the gravel beach helps avoid staggering to pass the overhanging willow this time. Moving up beyond the previous high point opens up a cast towards a pinch-point at the head of the pool between opposing sets of tree-roots on each bank.

In contrast to the soft sandy soil of the banks, those roots are not in any hurry to erode -so the river must squirt through that bottleneck after heavy rain and dig downwards to create depth on the left of the channel as I look upstream. Where that scoured bed material has been chucked up out of the deep hole and dropped towards my bank is what allows me to stand only calf-deep (instead of being over head-depth).

Casting up towards the pinch point and the cheb doesn't have time to hit the bottom as it is grabbed on the drop by a perch that is bigger, again, than the previous one. This fish thumps the rod tip over and the reel pays a little line out on a couple of the bigger kicks while I'm working the fish back downstream towards the net. It churns the water up in a white foam as it thrashes the final few feet over the rim of the net.

With one eye on trying to avoid disturbing any remaining fish in the shoal, I take the net with the mesh still submerged the few yards downstream to the gravel bar. Just as I get to a spot with the perfect depth of water, the sun creeps around into a gap in the vegetation and lights up this jewel of a fish pictured below. That sunlight shining through the molten glass-like translucent pectoral fin was just gorgeous. I've never seen a perch fin look like that before - with each individual ray picked out perfectly. Of course the blood red to orange fins are a classic feature of perch - but the almost UV-blue speckled sheen on the flanks of a perch is another thing that I was paying proper attention to for the first time.

Perhaps that's the coolest thing about using a camera; it really encourages you to look closely at some really beautiful things that we easily miss when we're just focused on only the fishing itself.

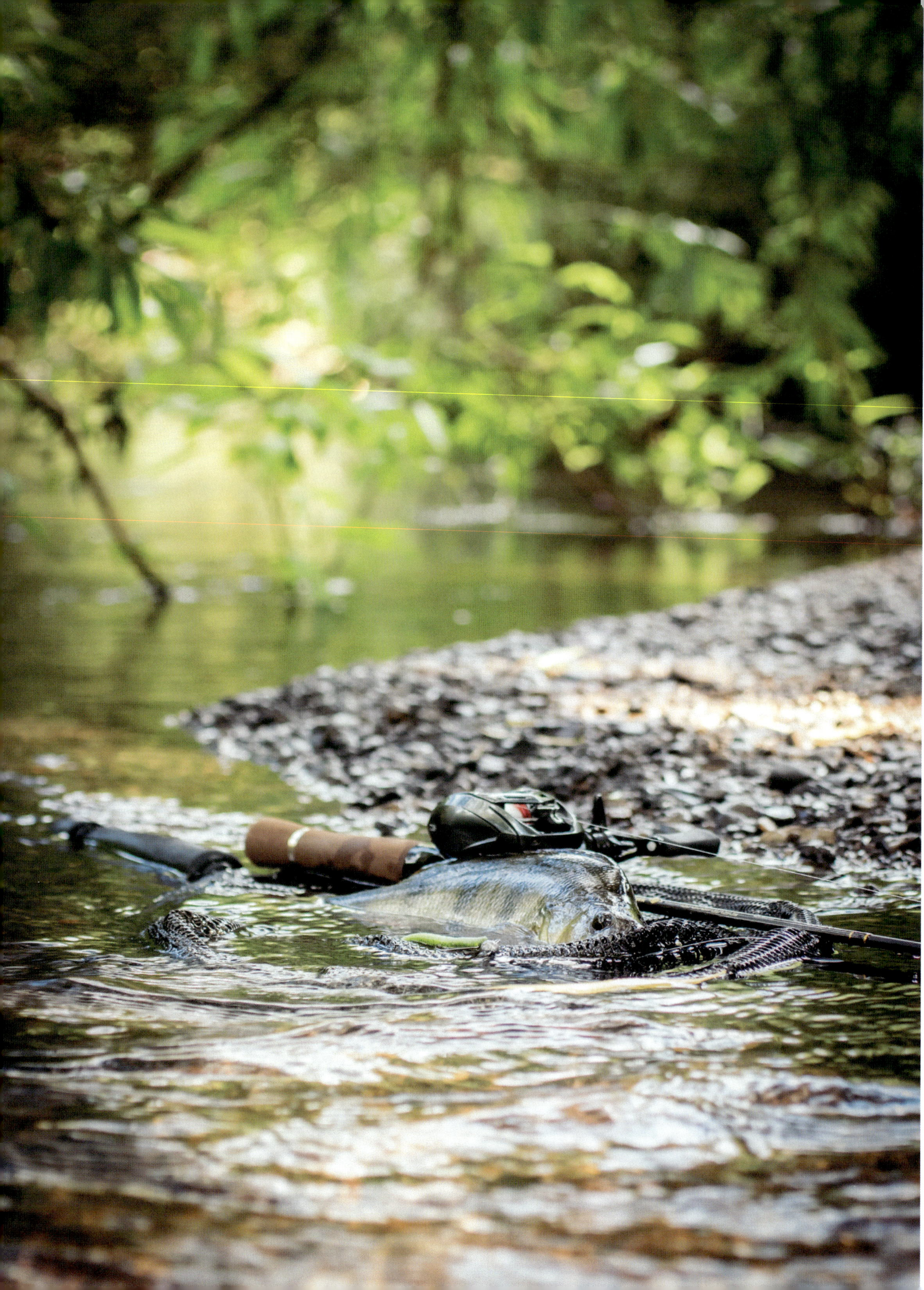

"Only, the snag started to shake its head..."

Maybe three casts after returning the previous fish, my little private slice of mystery stream gave up a lovely, solid perch of an improbable size for such a small river. It had that high-ridged back that reminds me of the hump-backed males of some pacific salmon species as they come into breeding condition.

A flat-trajectory flick right up into the pinch point let me trundle and bumble the busy stick-bait back up the sloping shelf towards my feet. The fish hit after following it maybe two thirds of the way back in - with not much more of a rattle than that first tiny fish. Setting the hook was a surprise - since I first thought I'd missed the fish and pulled the hook into a snag.

Only the snag started to shake its head and thump the rod tip. Another quite short, rolling, boiling, fussing fight ended with me bundling this perch into the net and feeling totally elated.

I took it back to the gravel bar to photograph among the overhanging willows and between the sunbeams and to try to place that fantastic creature in surroundings that did it justice.

As much as the fish itself was a wonderful reward, the place and the timing really magnified that enjoyment. I'd briefly escaped the stresses of a working day, been disappointed to find I couldn't fish my familiar spot where I knew I would be able to unwind for a couple of hours. Then by being forced to gamble and explore, I'd found a private, secret section of stream all to myself - like discovering a room in your house you never knew was there.

What's more it turned out to hold fish - and not only were those fish one of my favourite species, there were little ones that reminded me of childhood fishing joy, medium sized ones that would have made my juvenile-self jealous and then a perch that may as well have been a real life dragon to that same kid (the existence of either seeming equally unlikely).

It's such a perfect experience to explore a hidden, overgrown and secret paradise like that with a BFS rig.

A recipe for perfect happiness.

Photo: Tsurinan

Mountain Stream Adventures in the Japanese homeland of BFS with "Tsurinan-Desu"

YouTube: Tsurinan (Translation: "What is Fishing")

Tsurinan is the YouTube name of one of my favourite anglers. He fishes the remote mountain streams and ocean of the Tohoku region in the northeast of Japan's main island while recording his adventures on video for us to enjoy and learn from. This sort of direct-access to the practice and enjoyment of the sport in the settings where the term "Bait Finesse System" was coined is really valuable - so I'm delighted to feature his contributions here.

It's hard to imagine and understand the Japanese "Mountain Culture" of foraging, hiking, rough-camping and waterfall climbing that is attached to the various styles of fishing that are carried out in the mountain ranges of Japan without seeing or doing it first hand. So video, photos and stories are really important ways of sharing our fishing experiences across cultures. It also gives great insight into exactly where all the cool Japanese gear and lures come from too!

Photo: Tsurinan

Iwana or White-spotted char
Salvelinus leucomaenis
Photo: Tsurinan

Photo: Tsurinan

Can you tell me about Tohoku please?

The Tohoku region of Japan is located far from the metropolitan area and is a land rich in nature.

And since it snows a lot in winter, there is plenty of water flowing out of the mountains, and I think it is a land with the best conditions for trout.

Since it is a countryside, there are few anglers, and I think it is a land where it is relatively easy to catch fish.

Author note : *Angling is so popular in Japan that the fishing can be extremely difficult due to the angling traffic which streams experience (there is also a high proportion of catch and kill angling - though BFS anglers are big on catch and release with barbless hooks). To be able to find remote and less-visited wild streams is a very precious resource - and even in those cases many anglers will find the fishing technically very demanding with spooky fish in clear water.*

In genryu fishing, the angler is always seeking to reach the "sakana-dome" (fish-stopping waterfall - above which no fish have colonised). In a mountain angling joke, the limit of where you need to leave your vehicle on a dirt track and start hiking is called the "kuruma-dome" or car-stopping obstacle/limit.

What or who was your inspiration to pursue fishing in Japanese mountain streams (known as keiryu and genryu in Japan)?

I learned fishing from my father when I was a kid.

However, it was fishing with live bait and not with lures.

I studied by looking at fishing magazines and started lure fishing by myself when I was in junior high school.

I have been fishing for about 30 years, but I started to distribute fishing videos on YouTube in order to let many people know that knowledge.

Yamame trout (*Oncorhynchus masou*) Photo: Tsurinan

How (and when) did you discover BFS fishing?
I started when I learned about it on the Internet around 2017.

Until then, I had been doing lure fishing with spinning reels since I was a kid.

Author's note: *Genryū* (源流) *are the headwater streams of Japanese mountains. By popular definition, these also have to be difficult to reach - taking several hours to perhaps as long as several days to hike into from the nearest road access point. Because of the geography of the relatively short distance from mountain-top to sea, Japanese rivers are* **very steep**. *Their waters originate from snow-melt (which continues well into late spring) and this combination can make them very deep and very powerful even while they are still relatively narrow.*

People from outside Japan who enjoy "blue-lining" and exploring headwater streams often make the mistake of thinking that Japanese **genryū** *are small, benign trickles of water. In fact their surprising depth and power make them very dangerous areas to fish - particularly when coupled with how common land-slides and earthquakes are in Japan.*

Keiryū (渓流) *are, technically the "medium sized" mountain rivers (and sit between* **genryū** *and the large, intimidating* **honryū** (本流) *mountain rivers). However they are very commonly the same size as* **genryū** *streams; but are just easier to reach without as much hiking, scrambling and waterfall climbing (sawanobori). Elsewhere in the book, I'll use the shorthand, informal "genryu" English character spelling - but it should still be read with the long "ū" sound...*

Why do you enjoy Genryu fishing with BFS?

Fishing with baitcasting reels makes it easy to handle and easy to control your cast.

It is a highly suitable fishing method for accurately throwing lures into small spots in narrow mountain streams.

I am convinced that it is an effective fishing method for the headwater stream environment for which it was designed.

Photo: Tsurinan

What factors make "sinking minnows" good for your style of fishing?

In mountain streams, fish are often lying deeper in the water towards the bottom of the river.

And the sinking minnow is heavy, so it flies well when you cast it (as well as sinking easily to reach the fish).

You can catch not only near the bottom of the river, but also the middle depth-range with rod action.

It is attractive that you can enjoy fishing efficiently (**Author's note:** i.e. *creating efficiency by your casting coverage, ability to hit the feeding depth quickly - even in fast water - and also by the ability to cover multiple feeding depths via the "up and down" action of sinking and strong jigging with the rod tip.*

Smith D-Contact lures (left) are 50-mm long and weigh an impressive 4.5g. These are great for casting when paired with quite fast-action BFS rods. Plus they punch through fast surface currents, have a shimmying action while sinking and quite a wild inertia slide when twitched.

Photo: Tsurinan

Photo: Tsurinan

Author's note: *Particularly for cold water, as well as the heavy sinking minnows (e.g. Jackall Timon Tricoroll MAI 45 above) you will often see examples on Tsurinan-desu Channel videos of using Smith's "Bottom Knock Swimmer II" (BKS II; below) which is quite a radical bait sporting a highly exaggerated vertical jigging action - even when cast a good distance away from the angler.*

This presentation is achieved with a buoyant tail end and a heavy sinking head. When pulled, the BKS flares upwards, and when paused sinks vertically, head-down. The buoyant back end helps to keep the treble hooks (favoured by many anglers in the specific targeting of very difficult fish) clear of the riverbed rocks.

Photo: Tsurinan

23

What is your favourite retrieve for fishing sinking minnow (and why)?

Minnows and particularly heavy, sinking minnows make extensive use of twitch action.

I am good at hooking fish by making time to twitch violently to excite the trout and encourage them to eat it with a large up and down action of the rod and lure.

Iwana Photo: Tsurinan

What would you like to tell everyone about BFS?
Trout bait finesse fishing may overtake trout fishing on spinning reels in the future. In recent years, BFS exploded in popularity for Japanese trout fishing. This is because it is so easy that, with a little practice you will not want to return to using a spinning reel. This style of fishing is recommended for those who want to start lure fishing in the future.

Bait Finesse Reel Tour

There is no denying that one of the absolutely core parts of the BFS experience is the reel at the heart of your rig.

Obviously there are some wonderful top of the range options out there - and that is great to see alongside some of the crazy reel modders' tune ups and cosmetic upgrades

At the same time, there is no longer an exclusion from the "Bait Finesse Club" (compared to any other branch of regular angling) because of gear prices.

So let's have a look over just some of the options out there at the time of writing.

Oh, and then to go really deep on any or all of these reels, just scroll down the items under the Lure Hub menu on **fishingdiscoveries.com**

Affordable good looks with the ability to throw lures of genuine BFS weights (2.5g feels comfortable to cast)

KastKing Zephyr
(available with or without clicking drag)

Daiwa Air Stream Custom
(Clicking drag)

A genuinely stunning reel with fantastic small-stream accuracy performance. Worthy of a cult following

The Ship of Theseus or Ambassadeur 2500C?

There is a classic philosophy puzzle where you consider Theseus setting out from Crete in a wooden ship for his return to Athens. Over the course of a rough voyage, every single plank and oar comes to be replaced by new wood collected at each island stopover.

In the ancient version of this riddle, we are asked whether the object that arrives in Athens is still the Ship of Theseus or not - given that every single one of its components has been replaced?

A more modern update introduces a further conundrum - whereby each of the old components of the ship were stored in the hold throughout the journey.

At the end of the voyage - which is the *real* Ship of Theseus? Is it the vessel which did not exist at all at when Theseus left Crete; or is it the pile of broken, unusable but original pieces?

You could ask the same thing of my 1977 Ambassadeur reel; the Japanese BFS super-tuning components versus the bag of cogs, handles and other leftover bits bagged up in an office drawer...

Shimano Aldebaran BFS XG 2016
(Clicking drag)

FTB Brakes, extra magnets and Avail Microcast Spool

While it is far from the first BFS-style reel, the Aldebaran BFS 2016 deserves recognition as a milestone in Bait Finesse System fishing. *It is also always worth remembering that Shimano started promoting "BFS" in the first place.*

At the time hailed as the lightest reel Shimano had ever made and, with the advent of the after-market ultralight spool from Avail, it became the benchmark for casting performance with lures as light as one gram.

In other words, a lure so light that conventional wisdom would label it impossible to cast with a baitcasting reel.

That was a genuinely significant development with respect to countering the idea that

"*You'd better use a spinning reel*"

Shimano Calcutta Conquest BFS HG 2017
(Clicking drag)

Most people are surprised at how small the BFS version of the Calcutta is - given the familiar round baitcaster shape adopted by other reels in Shimano's Calcutta range.

In the above shot, I balanced a one penny coin (20.3mm diameter) on top of the reel body above the spool to give an idea of scale.

The solidity of the engineering and precision tolerances shine through in this reel - along with its stunning looks for fans of the round reel.

Since its introduction it has become an absolute staple of many aspiring BFS angler's kit list.

Custom wooden handle knobs look pretty cool on the Calcutta BFS 2017 especially when in use on-stream.

Daiwa Alphas Air TW 2020
(Non-Clicking drag as standard)

Widely reported as being the best BFS reel for casting lures down to 1-g (or even less) right out of the box with no further modifications needed.

My own experiences agree with this assessment when comparing to the Aldebaran 2016 with Avail spool upgrade (another reel often mentioned in relation to casting lures that light).

The ultra-light Roro AX24 spool is available in "standard" (4.6g; above) or "thicken" (4.9g) brake-inductor options for the Alphas and Steez Air TW 20. These are ridiculously light and amazing for flat-trajectory casts with the lightest of lures.

For the clicking drag experience, Ryan Sagisi of Sagisi customs has created two versions for the Alphas Air TW 20, the original (left) and the newer, improved manufacturing process version (right) below.

Fishband GH100
(Non-Clicking drag)

This was the first budget BFS reel that caught my attention (after The Reel Test's YouTube Review and remarkable casting results). Fishband certainly seem to have looked at reels like the Aldebaran and then found ways to make an affordable Bait Finesse Reel.

While it definitely benefits from having replacement bearings (basic ceramic hybrid bearings transform this reel), the experiences you can have on stream with light lures of around 2.5g and above are really fun.

In common with other reels at this price-point, if you get a backlash, loops of line will migrate behind the spool side-plates given half a chance.

Also, there do seem to be differences in how well the dynamic brakes perform between right hand and left hand versions (with the right hand wind reported to perform better than the left).

The orange shield on replacement bearings is visible in the brake plate (above) containing the Fishband reproduction of Shimano's original FTB (Finesse Tuned Brake) system of dynamic casting brakes.

Fishband PW100 Plus
(Clicking drag)

This second iteration of the PW100 comes with a MUCH lighter spool than the GH100 and the static style brakes should work equally well for right hand or left hand wind. Additionally, a clicking drag comes as standard. In my experience, it casts a lot better than the GH100 when comparing straight out of the box.

Fishband Clamber Hyper Micro CRHM06
(Clicking drag)

Modelled on a very similar platform to the PW100, the Clamber Hyper Micro has an aluminium body where the PW100 is carbon/plastic. With an exceptionally light stock spool and much finer tolerances between spool and reel-body, this is a higher priced offering from Fishband. I've not yet managed to trap my 4lb fluorocarbon behind this spool (whereas I've certainly done that on the PW100). Capable of casting lighter lures than the other budget reels featured here.

Bass & More with Chris "Anorak SZN"
Insta: @anorak_szn

Virginia, Washington DC Metro area,
Home waters local lakes, ponds, Potomac River & tributaries

Photo: Anorak SZN

How long have you been fishing in general and when/how did you discover BFS ?

I have been fishing since I was a child. My father is from Minnesota, so some of our most memorable times were fishing with him and visiting up north. I stepped away from it for a long time but got back into it after getting married and becoming more domesticated.

I discovered BFS by pure accident. I bought a house which, to my surprise, was located across the street from a lake. To my dismay, it was dredged, but around 2017 they filled and restocked it. The only problem was all of the fish in the lake were fingerlings, so the only fun to be had was on ultralight gear. I started to research ultralight fishing and finesse fishing and came across this website called finessfishing.com. The site was a treasure trove of information and opened my eyes to ultralight fishing and bait finesse - and not only that, the whole community was extremely open and helpful. I want to shout out the South East Asia enthusiasts, Europe as well as Russia for being that bridge in a sense from Japan to the USA. Brian Chan on Youtube was another resource that educated me early on, but countless experts and enthusiasts I have learned from along the way. It didn't take long before I went out and purchased a Kuying Teton and Aldebaran BFS shortly after that and never looked back.

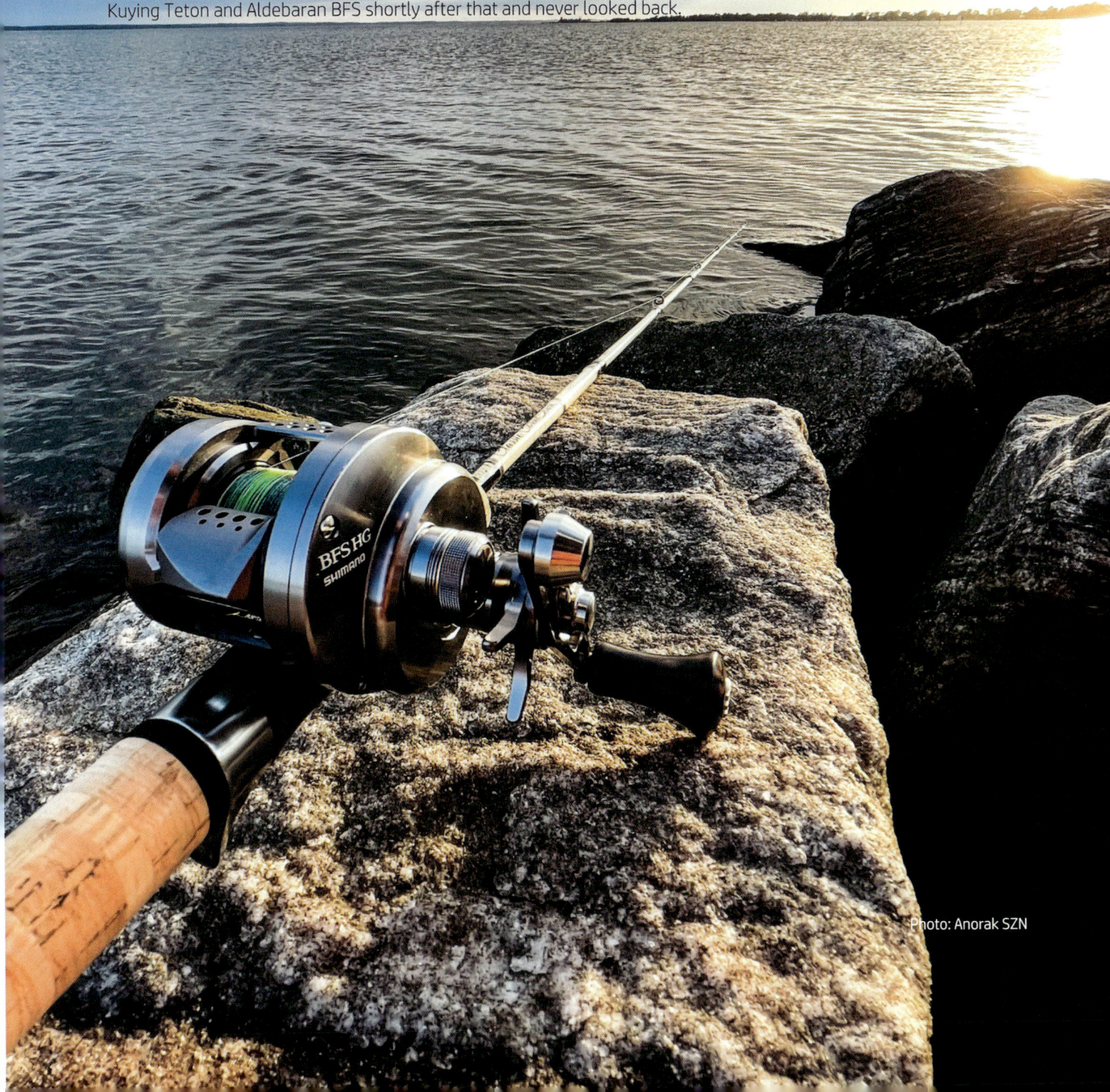

Photo: Anorak SZN

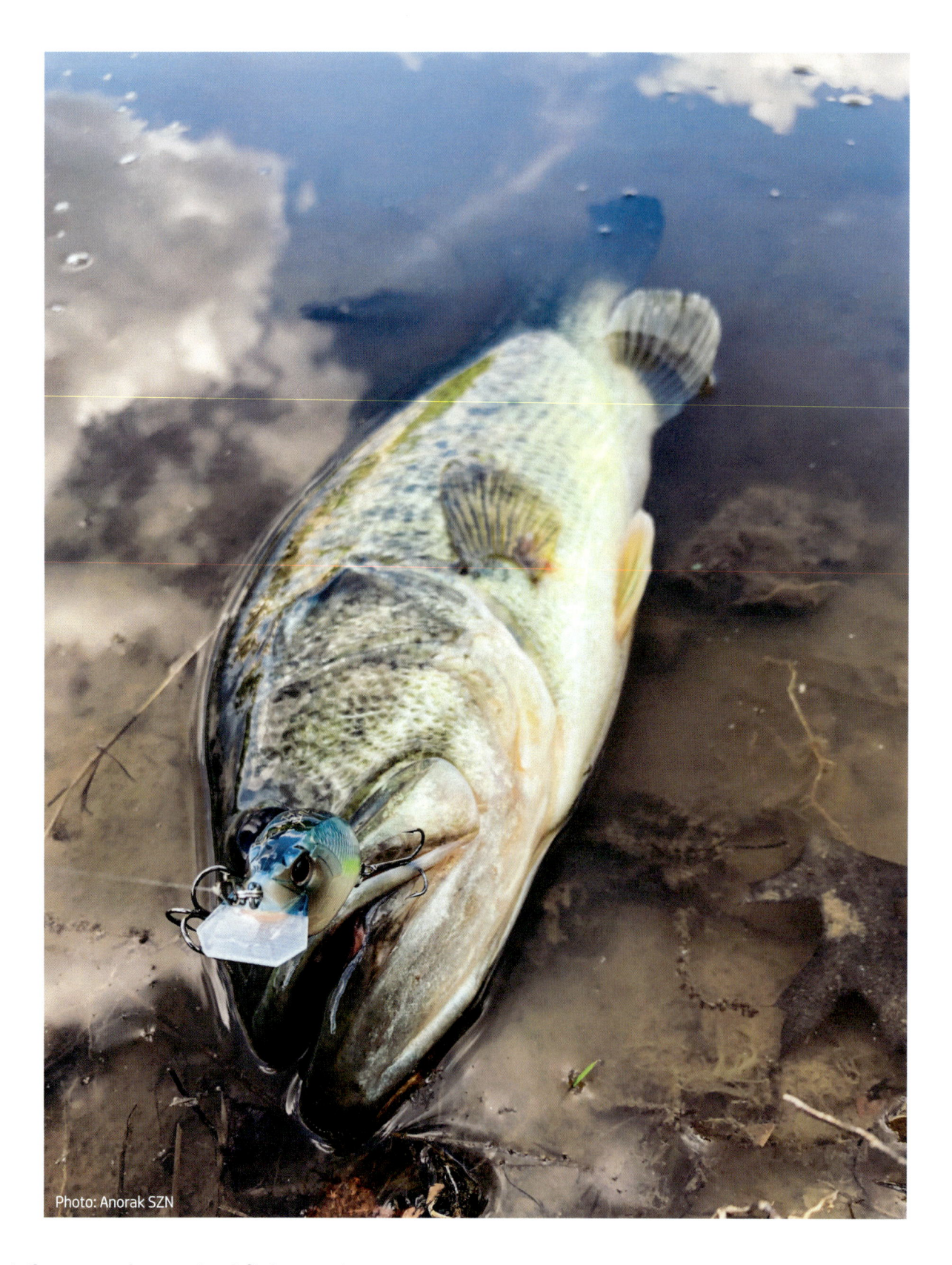

Photo: Anorak SZN

What are the typical fish species you target using BFS?
I target mainly largemouth bass, but when you throw lures of that size, they appeal to most fish. I throw the lure out, and whatever hits it hits it. Of course, it's always better to have appropriate size gear, but I fish for anything.

Quite a few Bass fishermen seem to feel that BFS is lame and not effective - what might they be missing out on (specifically in their bass fishing) if they never try BFS?

Bass fishing started in the USA as it is our native fish, so of course, there is always an apprehension to new techniques even when some of the best products and innovations have come out of Japan. I recalled stories of the drop shot floating around from Japan and the West Coast for years before it became a bass fishing staple.

Even the Ned rig faced pushback for years. BFS will catch on and be used when appropriate - and some folks really enjoy pushing the limits of how light a lure you can throw on a baitcaster.

My choice is entirely fun-oriented...I find that smaller baits get a bit more by more fish, increasing my chances of catching fish. I don't mind catching smaller species either. I love all kinds of fish. Maybe not the largest fish, but a two-pounder on light gear hits above its weight class. To me, it's about fun and enjoyment.

"Most Badass BFS rod & Reel...?"

What is your most badass BFS rod and reel combo right now?

It's not precisely a BFS reel, but I would say my Fenwick-Tiemco Aces 63UL "Bait Finesse Special" and my custom Rembrandt Reels Daiwa Steez CT SV TW 700SH. I throw baits in the 3-7 gram range on this rig. It can go lower and higher, but that is my functional range.

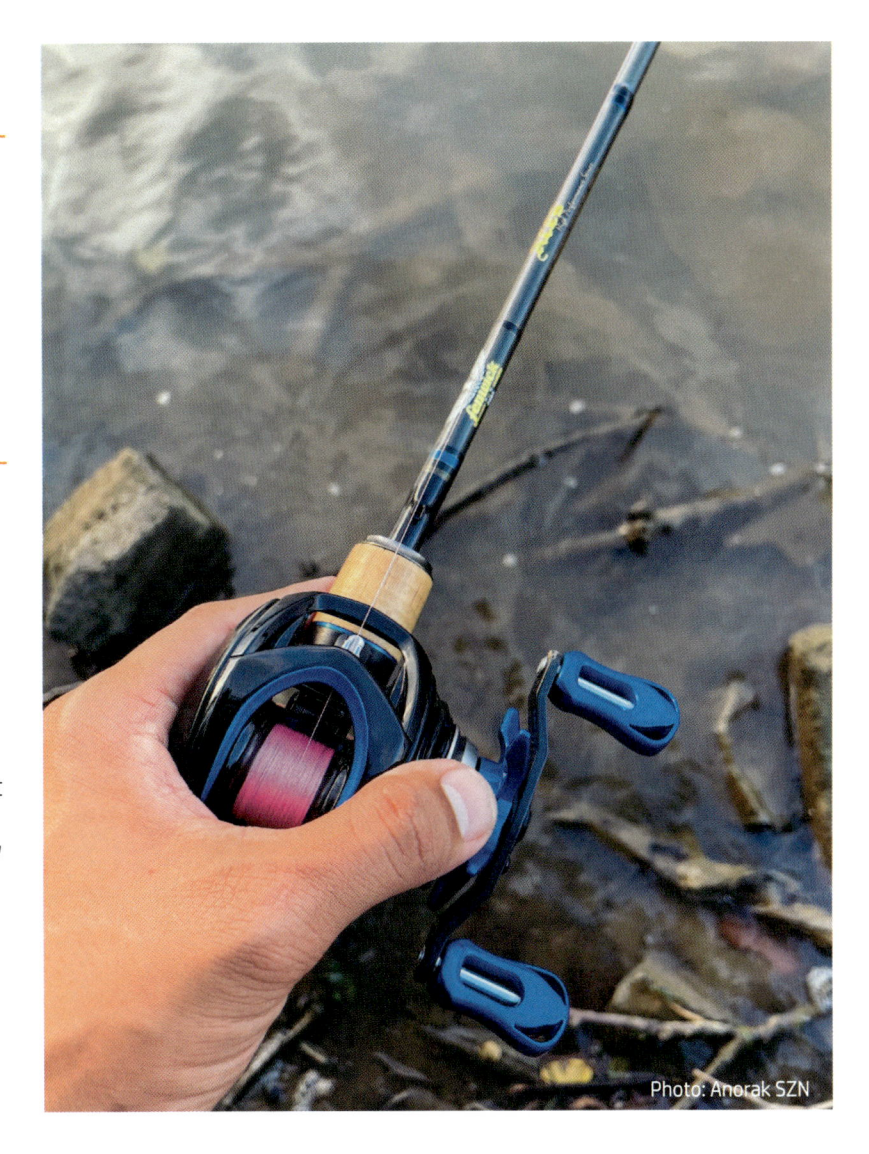

Photo: Anorak SZN

Tell me the story of your favorite/most memorable BFS trip, please!
I would say it was either early Spring 2019 when I had a healthy double-digit day, all ranging in the 2-3 pound range tossing a red craw Rapala Rippin Rap. It was pretty magical for an hour or so.

Or, maybe the time I caught an 8 pound (estimated) snakehead on the same Rippin Rap in Gold Chrome. That was intense. It was pretty touch and go, and the fish just refused to move for a short time. I had thought it came off or snagged, but it was sitting there. I almost pulled it until it started moving again. Fun stuff.

Photo: Anorak SZN

What's your favourite rig and tactics when targeting bass in warm conditions (and the same question for cold-water, early-season bassing)

In the warm season, I am throwing a free rig. In colder water more specially Fall or Spring, I am throwing a spinner bait or lipless crankbait. In winter I drop shot very light rigs.

Finesse Lipless Crank Photo: Anorak SZN

Bass on free-rigged creature bait Photo: Anorak SZN

What question should I have asked you already (but didn't) - and what would your answer be?

I can't think of one, but I would like to say I am fascinated by all styles of finesse fishing, be it target fish-specific or just a regional type of fishing. In different countries, they fish for other fish, but they also fish for the same fish in unique ways. I love seeing that and trying out these techniques for myself.

Do not be afraid to experiment. You can ask a million questions, but ultimately only you will be able to determine if something works...be it gear, lure, line, or rig. Enjoy what you do, and make memories out on the water.

Thanks!

Check out a 72-minute video diary of a summer-time trip to this stream PLUS bonus book-chapters in your exclusive owner's content (scan the QR code or type the link to register for free...)

fishingdiscoveries.com/bfs-book-accompanying-video-registration

BFS with Noodles on the Side

Recreating a Japanese BFS experience while exploring small streams at home

I don't care if people say it's cultural appropriation. You can't cancel how much I enjoy Japanese mountain culture.

I may not speak Japanese like a native - but I've done just enough fishing in the mountain streams of Japan to know that they "do" the social side of fishing 100% right over there.

The evenings of outdoor communal beers, BBQ (**yakiniku**) and foraged wild edibles (**sansai**/greens & **kinoko**/funghi) are at least as important as the fishing.

Ajari (ex-tournament bass angler & top tenkara angler) tends the camp BBQ

Foraged *sansai* tempura & soba noodles in a riverside car-park campground

Also, on the small stream keiryu or genryu day trips and overnighters, it probably won't all be fine-dining. More like instant noodles and the kind of improvised ingredient combos more commonly found in a cash-strapped student's recipe book. There will be cans of beer and super strength highballs though, that's not up for negotiation.

So when John and I met up to get some video of a day on-stream in the UK we both bring along very good memories of our trips to Japan to fish in mountain streams using traditional Japanese fly fishing methods. The settings and situations of those Japanese tenkara trips share almost everything with the origins of the BFS culture in Japan. The tribes of anglers have an awful lot in common. As well as the social side of things, there's the use of wet-wading gear borrowed from another outdoor pursuit of waterfall climbing (sawanobori). This is kind of canyoning in reverse i.e. wading and climbing upstream in the water as far as you can into the most inaccessible canyons of headwaters.

Putting on gaiter/knee-pads, neoprene socks and lightweight, streamlined, extra-grippy sawanobori style shoes is how I start my day with John on a small, wild, English trout stream in early summer. The ground next to where we've parked the cars is coated with a fine felt mat of beige, fluffy seeds from the surrounding trees. The stuff sticks to everything it touches - including the velcro fastenings covering the zip on my gaiters as I bend to tuck the zip shut against the springy stretch of the neoprene. It's a bit like dealing with spider web - since it sticks to hands just as easily as clothing.

There's a certain satisfaction of latching the metal keeper hook on the cuff of the gaiters into the laces of the sawanobori style shoes because it makes a dull click as the lace snugs home. Brushing off the cottony seeds makes sure I don't spoil that satisfaction. While the day is warm out here on the tarmac next to the path, the valley we are heading into is covered in trees with a high enough canopy to create a cool, mineral-smelling micro climate around the stream itself. Tramping down the forest track far enough to bring out a good sweat reveals a great reward. We've had some rain earlier in the week and water levels are looking good.

This is a rain-fed stream, running off peat-rich moorland, so the water is transparent - but also stained with rich beery tannins. While that is completely un-Japanese (the water would have to be aquamarine for that), it is a colour and style of trout stream that I absolutely love. Nice steep gradient full of current features, rocks, fallen tree stems, cold water and trout.

Today I've got the glass trout rod (Resilure Custom S-glass, 3-piece, 5ft rated 1-5g) and the Ship of Theseus Ambassadeur. I admit I indulged in buying a leather case for that reel - it seems to suit the spirit of the thing. I can't deny the ceremony of slipping the rod out of its aluminium tube strapped to my pack - coupled with the reverent unclasping and removal of reel from its religious-relic style case - well, it just feels good. That bit of needless theatre is a fun change from my usual scruffy, gaffer-taped-together gear and general disorganisation.

You can see the stone altar to the reel case, handy towel (a gift from a Japanese angling mentor) plus the **Waterclimb** brand wet wading gaitors/knee pads in full effect below:

Fishing begins and I'm both happy and nervous to win the coin toss and fish first (we tend to take turns pointing the camera at each other). At the moment the river still looks a little bit sleepy - so I don't really know what to expect in terms of fish encounters. Stepping into the cold water and having it flood the neoprene socks is a welcome slap that helps to wake me up. As a word to the wise, if you fancy trying wet wading in a trout stream - that generally means water cold enough to make your feet ache if you don't have neoprene socks. The difference in comfort they make is almost unbelievable and I've soon warmed up a nice insulating layer by wading to the tail of the pool I want to cast into first.

Major Craft Zoner Minnow 50 SP

The water is relatively shallow (with only the odd deeper scour pool) and fish have been willing to feed up in the water column recently. I also know that there will be some super shallow sections of flat water where a heavy bait slamming down on the surface could kill a whole pool. The glass rod, super ultralight spool and shallow trout stream mean I'm quickly reaching for the 2" Zoner Minnow suspending jerk bait from Major Craft.

In a perch colour it is also a pretty decent imitation of any young trout parr that might be hanging round and as long as the flow is not too powerful it is a great bait for subtle jerking as well as slow and fast rolling. The big factor helping my confidence in the flat shallow water is how gently you can put that bait down on the surface when everything goes right with your cast. I think this gives me many more chances at showing a fish my bait before spooking it. At the same time, the Zoner lands with enough of a plop to get a predator looking up to see what's what (and slamming that reaction bite).

A few casts around the tail of the pool saw no response and I moved upstream so that I could kneel down and throw into the main body of the pool. A straight cast would see me covering the margins of my own bank (to my left as I looked upstream). Equally I could throw diagonally right and hit the margins on the opposite bank - as well as retrieving back through the central water.

Almost straight away I had a good fish follow to nearly under my rod tip and roll on the lure. Several casts to the same spot saw no further response. Then, chucking diagonally up and across to the far bank another two fish snatched or boiled at the lure without hooking up. It was only when I switched into including really quite long pauses between each quarter turn of the reel handle that something slammed the minnow and stayed on. Although the hook pulled before I could actually land the fish, I definitely stored up that specific retrieve style as a good option. With those really light minnows, it is easy to overpower their action with too much rod tip motion and too savage a cranking style. In many ways, it is the complete opposite to the dense, sinking minnow approach where the rod tip action can be extremely agitated (as described by Tsurinan already). Instead, with a lightweight suspending jerk bait you usually need to be a bit more delicate. The quick quarter (or half) turn of the crank in a "turn-stop-turn-stop-turn-stop" sequence creates a kind of underwater "walk the dog" motion that you see with surface pencil baits. Some days, presenting that side profile to a following fish and having it hang there for a fraction of a second can cause spectacular hits. Other days, it's all about the constant wriggle that I guess gives the impression of a totally naïve baitfish having a swim through a bad neighbourhood (without realising the danger it is in).

Today, though, the real key seemed to be extending that stopped phase to much longer than normal - so that it lasted maybe around a second or slightly more. Hits would start to come either on the static, broadside pause or the trout would jump on the lure as it just started to move and "escape" right at the beginning of the next twitch.

One of the other things that I began to notice was, when the fish ran straight towards me, I had to crank really fast on the low-geared Ambassadeur to try to keep the line tight. The 1977 reel model I own has a gear ratio of 4.7:1 and that means your cranking hand needs to go some to keep up with a head-on charge from a trout. Picture the blurred speed of a bee's wing in flight and you're pretty much on the money. That being said, the forgiving and responsive action of the S-glass blank is actually very good at keeping a fish pinned in faster water. Sometimes a stiffer carbon blank might bounce a hook out if the fish zigs when the rod zags (though the flip side of that is the stiffer blank might also be better on hook-sets).

Moving through the pools and there was lots of action - including some shockingly big fish flashing at the lure before slinking away moodily under tree roots never to return for a second look. Yet, plenty of lovely fish stayed on long enough for us to say hello and maybe snap a photo or two.

The satisfaction of bending the glass rod into a fish matches so well with the feel of the beautiful engineering of that old round-reel. You definitely feel the full outfit come alive with a fish attached to the lure with it jagging against the rod-top. Couple that with the muted purr of the gears when winding against the weight of a fighting fish and the experience is about as good as it ever gets. A basic, lo-fi drag clicker adds to that old-school (and well-engineered feel).

It sounds like a cliché to say it - and it is still truer than for any other fishing situation I can think of - even without hooking a fish, this outfit is pure bliss to fish with. I enjoy all sorts of styles of fishing across so many types of gear (from fly to lure to bait fishing in fresh and saltwater). Yet some days all I want to do is go out and cast an ultralight baitcaster on a little wand of a rod. When that mood takes hold, I often find it very difficult to look past the glass rod and the old round reel. The flex of a loaded up glass blank sending a flat, smooth cast out across the stream feels like achieving a state of grace (at least when it goes right).

I blame Angler Saito.

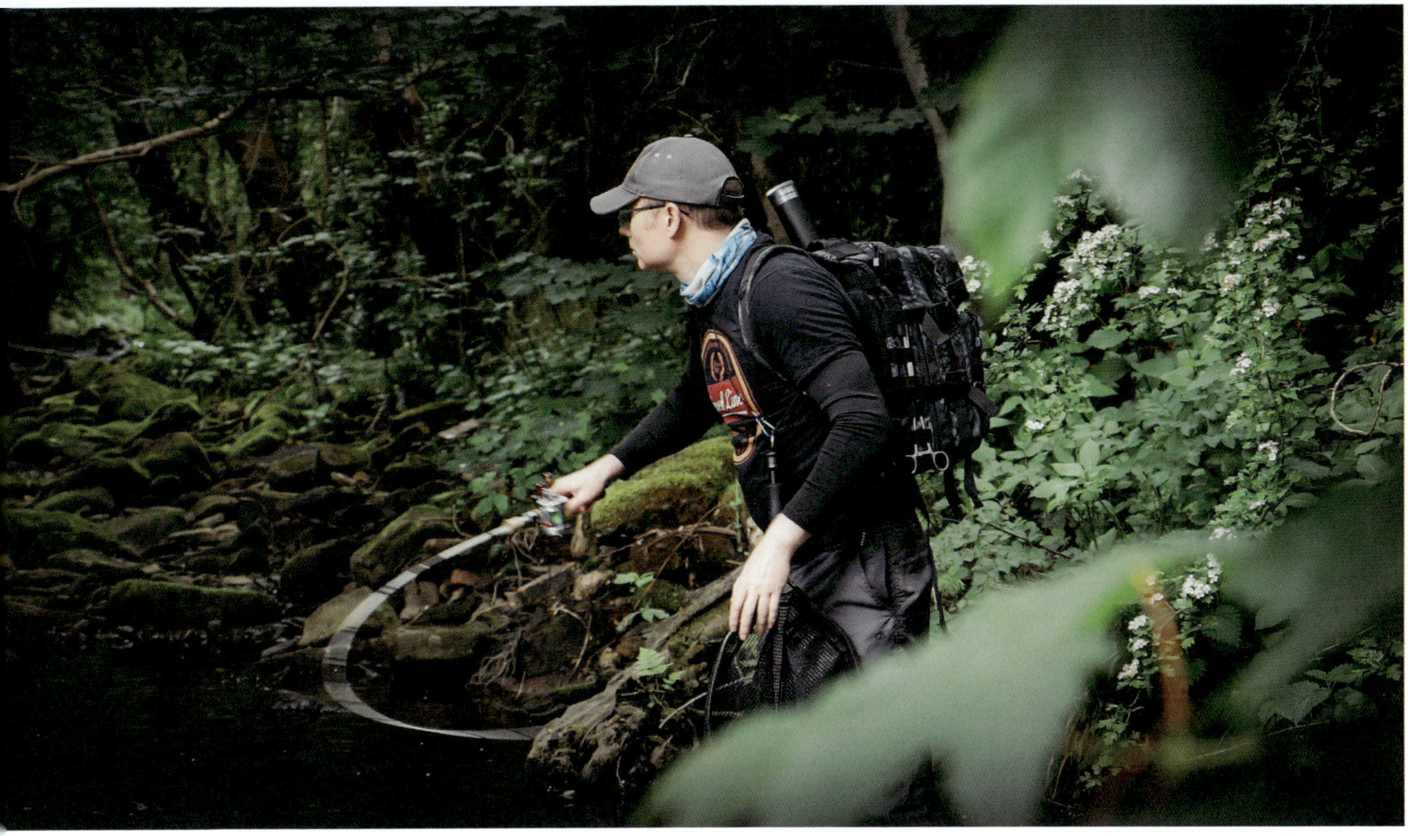

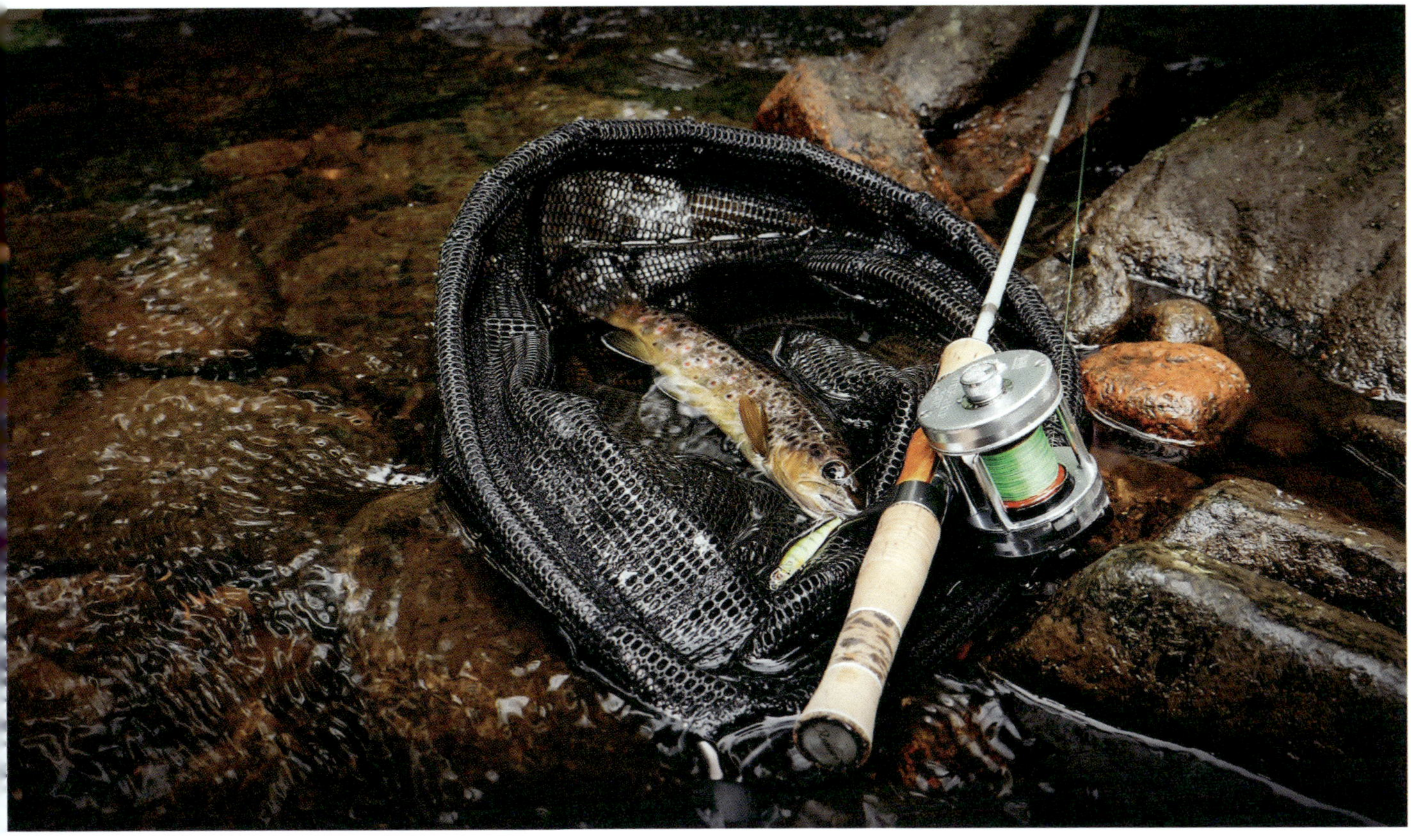

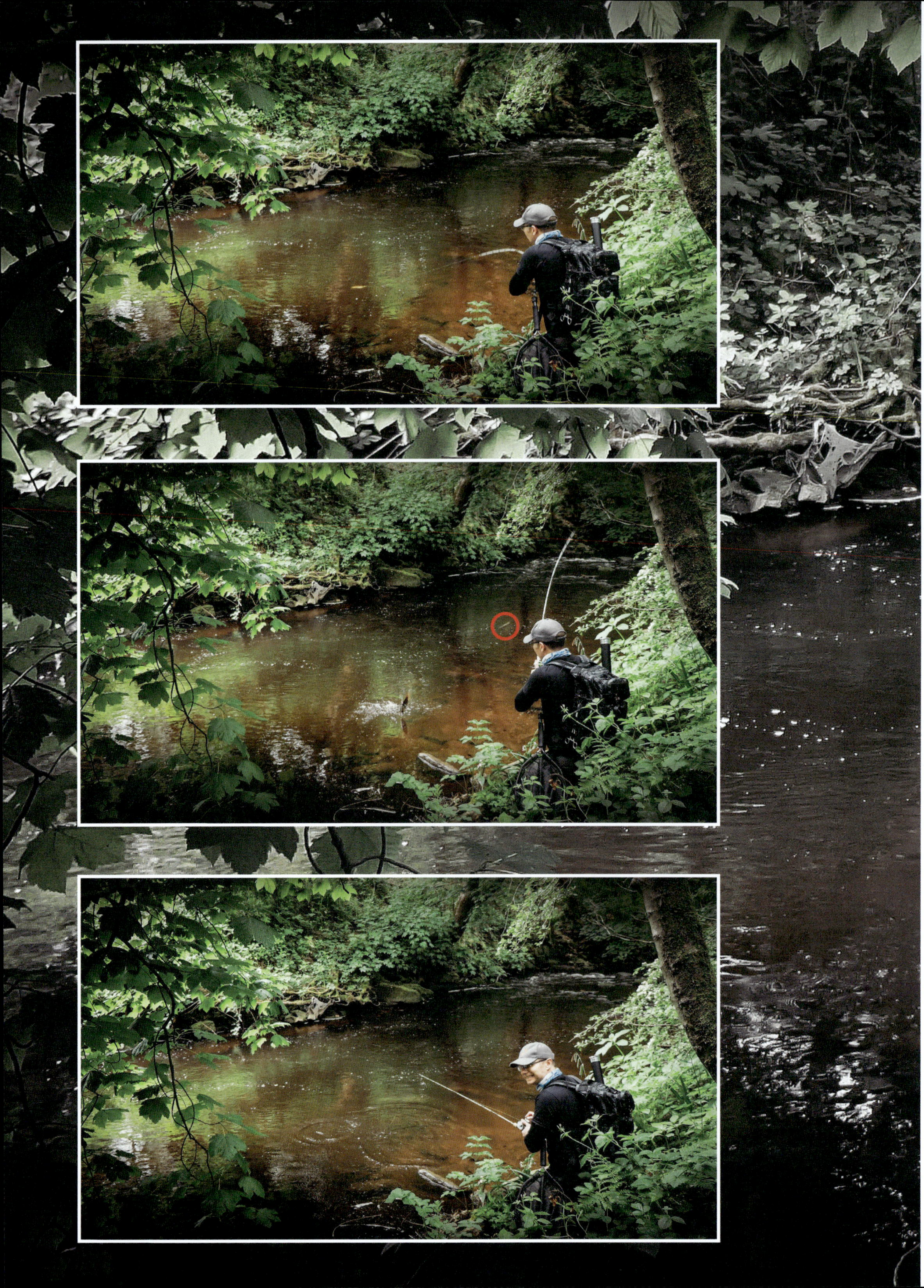

Long distance release

Although I probably would have preferred to land this fish (obviously!), the adrenaline from having it follow right back and then smash the lure almost under the rod tip before throwing the hook with a spectacular leap was quite something.

You can see the splash of the departing trout making its escape (below)

The middle picture on the left shows the lure flying through the air (circled in red) and suggests it's worth practicing a good old boxing slip to avoid taking a direct hit to the grill. The lure ended up in the bushes.

A rueful grin - well, OK, a grimace - and then back on with the job at hand of working the rest of this fantastic pool. There were at least three good fish at home around the features here - including the one leaping in the picture at the beginning of this chapter. That one, at least, was landed and admired briefly.

By the time I'd worked my way to the riffle upstream it was time to hand over to John.

But not before we'd fired up the Jetboil and cooked up some dirty instant cup noodles for lunch by the river.

MSR
ISOPRO
PREMIUM, ALL SEASON FUEL BLEND
ISOBUTANE / PROPANE MIXTURE
CUP NOODLES
Soba
Wok Style
CUP NOODLES
Soba
Wok Style
YAKITORI CHICKEN

All garbage was packed out in bags

You can see (right) that John is *devastated* to be forced to hand over the camera and swap it for his Shimano Cardiff Native Special (4' 2") and Calcutta Conquest BFS combo.

Although still one of his earliest BFS outings, John's previous experience with baitcasters and also casting accuracy with many different styles of fishing let him quickly get into the swing of hitting spots tight up to the tree roots and bank-side rocks. That ability to cross-train is definitely a feature of fishing that we both enjoy and promote - since wherever you find yourself in the world it means you're never too far away from a fishing adventure. I actually enjoy watching through the viewfinder as he works up the cool, leafy corridor; picking away at likely spots. The short, UL rod is in its element on this small, lively stream in the woods.

The hits/near misses, fish that spit the lure and captures feel like a real team effort and I find that trying to capture some of the action through the lens is a little bit like striving to catch the fish themselves. The mindset and the things your brain is looking to interpret are very similar. Alright, I admit that doing the actual fishing is still that bit more exciting and satisfying - but catching images is a pretty decent substitute.

After starting out with the AliExpress floating minnow in the top picture, John soon switches to a Zoner in a pale ayu pattern. Even with the slightly heavier stock spool of the Calcutta, I can see him find his range with some neat roll casts. Right on cue, after dropping the lure into the prime lie of the current-break - just behind a submerged boulder (below the branch laying in the stream) - a good fish latches hold. On the little wand of a rod it is a spirited fight full of leaps and showers of spray. I'm really happy for John (while also healthily jealous of his capture) as he nets this one. It obviously grabbed the lure full across the body - since the single barbless front hook is right in the scissors of the jaw. As with all the fish we catch today, this wild trout is painted in stunning colours. The darker barring from its parr marks is still possible to see and this is another little reminder of the yamame and amago (*Oncorhynchus masou macrostomus*) trout we have caught in Japan (e.g. below). In those fish, the body barring is even stronger - but it is not something I see a lot of in brown trout from hatcheries and fish farms. Instead it seems to be something that comes out much more in some strains of wild brown trout in the UK. Having been a fly fisher for so many years, I thought it might seem a bit strange to target wild trout on lures. There is a strong element in British fly fishing suggesting lures are what poachers use after all. What I can now say is - perhaps owing to the finesse angling culture in Japan - it feels absolutely appropriate on BFS gear. The casting is, if anything, more difficult than the much-revered fly cast. Gear, stream-craft and the direct immersion in the tumbling streams are all every bit as subtle, delicate and complex as the lightest fly tackle.

Amago caught by John in Itoshiro, Japan

As we reluctantly pack up when we can no longer delay it any further, pushing our way through the undergrowth and tramping up onto the path the day feels complete. Another wonderful memory of an already rich archive of angling adventures is logged. Maybe we didn't hike for more than a day to get there (or climb any vertical waterfall faces), but the experience genuinely feels like a wonderful mixture of British and authentic Japanese BFS. *Wet-wading and cheap cup noodles by a steep woodland trout stream can do that to you…*

"Snakehead Heaven" Photo: Jimmy Ly

Snakeheads, Kayaks, Power BFS & the Multispecies Angling Experience with Jimmy Ly

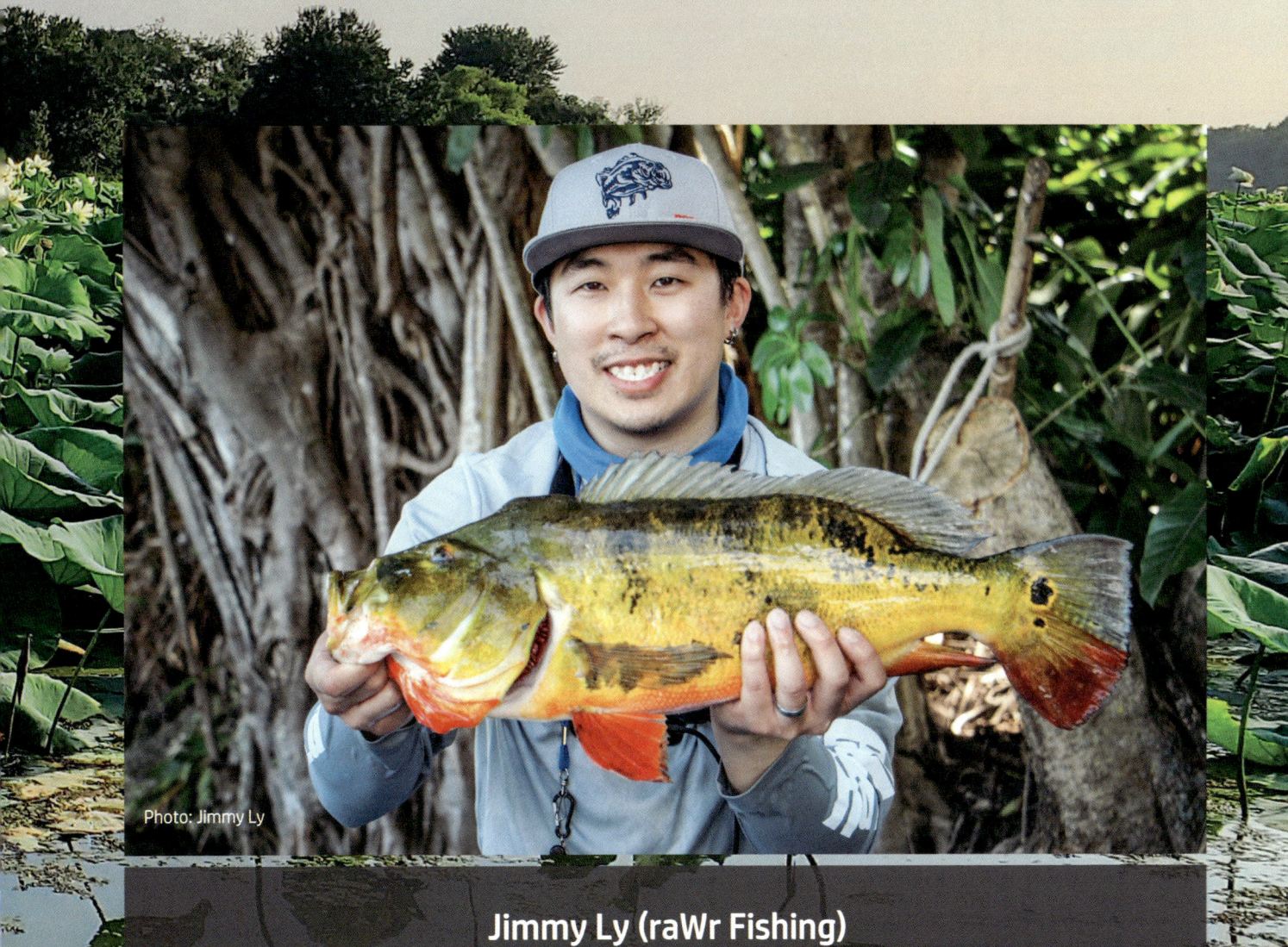

Photo: Jimmy Ly

Jimmy Ly (raWr Fishing)

Instagram: www.instagram.com/rawrfishing/
YouTube: www.youtube.com/rawr215/

I am currently 37 and live in New Jersey, right outside of the Philadelphia area in the US.

As a kid, I grew up in Philadelphia where street violence and drugs ravaged through the hoods. I lived there up until I was 12 before moving out of the city and into Delaware State... sounds like nowhere - but one great thing was having a tiny creek by my house!

Given that I had arrived at a new place with no friends, it was difficult to fit in - particularly being both new and different. Yes, I was a minority. Transferred into a school with less than 12 Asians, half of that were Indians, so that made me still look pretty much an oddball. On top of that, I don't look nor behave like other Asians. I came from the hood... enough said!

Since it was hard to fit in and I was being alienated (as well as being bullied), I resorted to video games and exploring the creek down the street with my siblings. I eventually convinced my father to get me a cheap Zebco rod from K-Mart and I made my way to catch creek chub, sucker fish and eels. That was where it all started. Hooked early before drugs could get to me. If I ever could get into the world of education, I would teach kids how to fish and would love to promote the very popular line here in New Jersey "Hooked on Fishing - Not Drugs". But since I am not in the field of education, I spread my knowledge, love and passion for fishing through my social media platforms. This is how I met Paul, who is on the other side of the ocean! Our passion coincided with each other and now I am answering some questions for Paul's book. Let the interview begin!

What is your fishing background before you got into BFS?

Growing up, I was primarily a bass fisherman (Largemouth/Smallmouth Bass). However, I am currently a multispecies angler targeting any fish that would bite small finesse lures, or anything that would want to destroy a topwater frog! For the most recent years, I have been targeting crappies, trout, bass, perch and snakeheads! People think topwater bass fishing is fun, they have to experience some snakehead fishing! Holy moly! Big explosions and a crazy deathroll on the surface!

Anyhow, as I was growing up, the internet wasn't big at that time - so I relied on magazines at the bookstore for my fishing knowledge. Given that the ocean was pretty far away and I didn't have a car as a kid, the magazines that I obtained were primarily bass fishing related. Even "In-Fisherman" magazines were mainly about bass, although they do pull in a few articles here and there about other fish.

Fast forward to post college (went to Drexel University, go Dragons!), I started my first job in New Jersey. Mind you it was 50 miles to get there and back. Along the way, there was so much water, so many places to fish! Eventually, my co-worker caught wind that I was a fisherman and introduced me to kayak fishing. From there, I was hooked!

In 2011 I got my first Kayak... a dingy... I explored some saltwater fishing since my co-worker was into that. Caught some nice flounder, stripers and other species, but it wasn't something I would be willing to do with my 8-foot kayak.

By Fall of 2012, I had bought my first house. I bought a new car in spring of 2013 along with a new fishing kayak. The focus was still bass fishing, but I quickly went into saltwater fishing. Nothing better than hooking up a 30 plus lb striped bass and letting it haul you around!!! Seriously!

Photo: Jimmy Ly

Then in 2015 I bought my next kayak.. the best of the BEST... a Hobie Outback. God I love this kayak and it's still treating me well! Less paddling and more fishing! Just pump them legs and off we go!

Now, after a few years of kayak fishing, I realized that I like to throw lighter lures. Why? Because kayak fishing is exhausting. Let me paint the picture for you. I am 5'5" and weighing around 140 to 190 (depending on the year you are asking :P). The kayak itself is about 80 lbs. But when rigged up, it is closer to 100! For a trip to happen, I first have to load the car, then the kayak. Now drive to a location, unload everything and if the launch location is far from the car (which is usually the case if I am saltwater fishing); then I have to wheel the kayak on its cart along with EVERYTHING to the water before taking the cart back to the car. Then it is fish on time! How long? mmm... depends how far I go! For some of my saltwater trips, I drive 2 hours... so I would have to be up 4 am, load the car and be out before sunrise! So yeah after fishing, reverse everything! Get home and then CLEANING TIME.. holy hell... it could be hours! I clean my kayak plus my gear if it was saltwater. Then if I brought fish home to eat (gotta keep the family happy sometimes), guess who has to do the cleaning? Yes.. that would be me too. As you can imagine, it is quite exhausting.

So I changed my style of fishing and went finesse. Lighter gear, lighter lures, light everything. I mean before I used to throw 3/8th to ½ oz lures for bass in heavy tackle. Imagine the milk crate full of tackle boxes and bags of lures. Now I am throwing things from 1/16th oz to ¼ oz. Much better and less tiring.

Photo: Jimmy Ly

I eventually hit a roadblock since I have been throwing light stuff on spinning setup and man I hate them line twists and wind knots. At that time, I didn't like how BFS tackle cost so much, but I said to myself... I don't need it... ehhhh maybe I do... let's fiddle with cheaper ones first!

Currently, the only fish I target using MH gear and above are snakeheads. Of course I still use finesse stuff for snakeheads (especially BFS), I just go for whatever bites using BFS and VFS (I will let Paul elaborate on that one!)

Can you tell me the story of how you discovered BFS - and your early experiences with it?

I discovered BFS from Tackle Tour Forums, then YouTube videos. I would say the first reel that caught my attention was the Aldebaran BFS 2016. Unfortunately, to import this reel at that time was ridiculous! For a light tackle reel, it shouldn't be more than 200 dollars even if it's a premium reel I'd say. But that's just my opinion! So I waited... until I saw someone (I think his name was Bobby Emmory on Instagram) and he had a Shallow Spool on a KastKing Spartacus.. Hey, I already got a KastKing Spartacus!!! Why not convert it to a BFS reel? Then after buying one spool off AliExpress, I became comfortable exploring other CDM reels on Aliexpress. All this started around the year of 2018.

Most of the CDM reels were terrible at the time. I was watching the Haibo Steed closely, but wasn't impressed. Since I was with KastKing as a Brand Ambassador at that time, I messaged their CMO many times and during meetings, I would ask for BFS reels. Their answer was that they don't see a market for it, especially in the US. But I never gave up! I said "You guys sell stuff in Asia that is marketed for them, why not BFS too?" Eventually I think I annoyed the crap out of them enough that they said write up a business/case study and let us take a look at it. So I wrote up a 6-page paper showing how BFS has changed from the early 2010s to the current date and the interest has skyrocketed in Asia. I compared products from Japan and China. I have shared videos from The Reel Test and more to KastKing and many other forum posts. I gave examples of what they should make for their first "Budget BFS" rod and reel. That very next summer of 2019, during ICAST (hosted in Florida), the CEO of KastKing, Tate Cui, messaged me on Facebook messenger with a photo of the KastKing MegaJaws BFS Prototype. He asked for my address so I could test it and provide feedback. After fishing it a few times, I wrote with a ton of info to Tate as well as convincing him to let me portray it publicly on YouTube for the community to provide feedback as well. Nine months later, I got the first official BFS rod/reel combo released in Asia, the KastKing Zephyr BFS!!!

As of the summer of 2021, I am no longer a KastKing Brand Ambassador. Life caught up with me and I have not much time to fulfill my obligations as a team member. I left KastKing on good terms and with a good relationship so that I can continue to work with them to grow their presence in the BFS community. I can't wait to test and help create more products with KastKing!

Taking a step back, 2020 was probably my best time with BFS. Why? Because I bought my first JDM BFS reel, the Daiwa Alphas Air TW (**right**). In addition, I had two fans sending me some BFS stuff as well! Ruda from Croatia sent me the Tsurinoya Dragon C702L. This is a 7 ft rod Light action. He said he had watched many of my older videos and said this would fit my fishing better than my other rods. He was absolutely right! So correct that I bought another one for my younger brother, who is my fishing partner in crime! The second gift from a fan was even more epic... the Shimano Adebaran BFS XG 2016!

As you can see, my experience hasn't been long, but I have made a ton of BFS content since 2018. I portrayed my exploration of BFS starting with the KastKing Spartacus, to many CDM brands and now JDM reels! I don't see myself stopping anytime soon as my love for finesse fishing has just grown even stronger!

Here are some of the reels I have played with and my thoughts:

Tsurinoya XF50 - this isn't really a BFS reel, but a long cast reel with some BFS capabilities. I don't really recommend it for UL or Light Tackle BFS Fishing, but it was my 2nd finesse baitcasting reel that I have obtained for BFS purposes. I soon swapped out the stock spool with the Tsurinoya Spirit Fox BFS reel as it fit and it became wonderful! If you have a stock XF 50, it would be best a Power BFS Reel (To be covered on the next interview question)

Fishband GH100 - Probably the worst performing reel I have gotten to date. My first official BFS reel is a Shimano Aldebaran copycat. They wanted to utilize the Shimano FTB Braking system (Finesse Tune Braking) as it was one of the best braking system for BFS reels. The spool was heavy, the bearings were terrible and caked with grease and dust. Even with micro bearings swapped, the brakes just didn't want to work. I really wanted to like it since I didn't have the Shimano Aldebaran at that time, but it was so bad I had to put it on the side. Not all copies can replicate the original!

Tsurinoya Spirit Fox - After swapping spools on the XF-50 with this reel's spool (you can message Tsurinoya on Aliexpress to purchase spare parts) I have come to like my XF-50. With that said, I have decided to buy the Spirit Fox BFS reel and fish it. I have upgraded the bearings as well as it was a perfect time to dabble with micro bearings. I quickly learned that EVERY BFS REEL SHOULD HAVE MICRO BEARINGS OUT OF THE BOX. sorry for the caps... Also note that there is a new Spirit Fox with a lighter spool that has been released in 2020, but I have yet to play with it. Overall, I feel that this is a great reel and is comparable to the KastKing Zephyr BFS reel for price and performance.

Tsurinoya Dark Wolf - This is a reel (right) that copied the Shimano FTB Braking system. It cast pretty well, but it was unfortunate that I cannot get the spool pin out to replace the bearing. This reel, like most CDM reels who copied the FTB Braking, suffers from a weak braking system. This isn't a problem for most people though unless you plan on skipping heavier BFS lures.

Photo: Jimmy Ly

Kyorim Black Knight - Another FTB Braking reel with the weakest brakes. It is also the worst quality! One of my local fans bought it and threw it out. Another one gave it to me to do a review.. my god.. Right out of the box and the plastic body fell apart easily and the spool pin doesn't even stay in - it slides all over the place! Although it cast a long way due to the weaker brakes, it was definitely a bad reel. But at least it cast further than the GH100!

Shimano Aldebaran BFS XG - King all rounder BFS reel! Comes already with micro bearings and can cast down to 1 gram if you put on a thin diameter line. It won't be that far, without an aftermarket spool swap, but it can get out better than all the CDM BFS Reels by far! But you would excel casting heavier lures as Shimano reels are made for bass fishing.

Daiwa Alphas Air TW 2020 - King of UL BFS that can cast down to 1 gram out of the box relatively far. My favorite reel to date for trout and panfish. Now in the BFS realm, there's really only two categories.. BFS (very vague) and Power BFS (still vague). If there is a way to break the classifications down further, I would say this is an UL BFS reel.

Shimano Curado BFS (left) - I hate to say this... but I feel that this reel finally came to the North American and European Market due to the KastKing Zephyr BFS reel going global. So could it be said that Jimbo was the reason that this reel was released globally? Maybe - but let me tell you, my intention of having KastKing bring BFS tackle global was to push the Japanese companies to go global as well. And that happened! Woohoo! Now this spool is heavier than the Alde and many other good BFS reels, but I feel that it's perfect! Why? The fish that are most popular in North America are bass! Largemouth and smallmouth bass... Most bass anglers would throw lures 3 grams and up anyway and this reel will do perfectly fine! I have seen many US anglers use this reel as a

Photo: Jimmy Ly

way to flip and pitch short distances.. Not my cup of tea, but as long as they use it, the BFS Niche is growing! I hope to see Daiwa jump in for 2022!

Which fish species and what are the main rigs/baits you tend to focus on across your BFS fishing?

As a multi species angler, I target anything that bites. I am extremely happy to catch a panfish such as a bluegill or a crappie. But if a bass bites or a pickerel bites, I'll be happy too. If it wasn't for social media, I would just use a 1/16th oz Jig and a 2 to 3 inch grubtail and that's it. With that said, I am on a journey to grow on social media - and means I also have to "fish for likes". That is how your account grows, which means I will have a bigger audience and I can influence a larger amount of folks.

Eurotackle Z-Viber Micro Photo: Jimmy Ly

Long story short, outside of simple jigs, I fish anything that is small and trendy in that moment. Seems like I have been hooked on Eurotackle and their B-Vibe swimbaits the longest. Other lures I am currently exploring are JDM and CDM lures that are being carried at Bait Finesse Empire. This is a US Based store that focuses on selling BFS tackle and finesse lures.

Now there is actually one species of fish that I do target for using mainly heavy tackle and that is the Northern Snakehead. But I also use finesse tackle to target these fish as it is very fun and challenging. Because they have a super strong bite force and a hard bony jaw, it is a bit difficult to set the hook with small thin hooks and flimsy rods. They would also bend your hooks pretty badly, so I would target these fish using some bigger finesse lures, which calls for Power BFS!

What is "power BFS" - and where is the boundary between "power" and "regular" BFS for you?

I know there is an unofficial definition within the BFS community that will tell you a specific weight range would be considered BFS and then there is Power BFS. Let me tell you this right off the bat... I don't know that range in my head, but I am sure Paul would be able to tell you what the majority of anglers within the BFS community have agreed upon. I do understand why it was created as it would be helpful for folks to teach other folks and share gears easier, but the downside is that there are so many folks that would marry themselves to numbers. To me, that means you are creating boundaries and locking yourself in.

I really hate boundaries. Some would say Bruce Lee is the father of mixed martial arts. During his time and even before his time, most martial artists were LOYAL to the style they have chosen. Bruce Lee hated that and saw that all forms of martial arts have their pros and cons. So he took the best of every martial art that works for him and used it. From there, he even developed his own philosophy of martial arts and also made the world acknowledge that martial arts are not just Karate (which was crazily hot at that time).

To me, if you use a BFS reel, it's BFS. If you use an Ultralight and Light action rod, that's your general BFS as this style of fishing is normally associated with the most finesse lures possible. Yes, very vague, which is why people want to see a range. If you need to force a number out of my mouth, that would be 7 grams and below.

For Power BFS, it can be anything from 3.5 grams and above. As you see, there is an overlap, but the key difference between your general/regular BFS to Power BFS lies in the power/action of the rod and the strength of the line.

TLDR (too long didn't read) version;

A super easy way for me to help define BFS vs Power BFS would be the fishing rod! A fishing rod will tell you exactly what lure and line ranges you can use right? With that said, I consider what most people think of regular BFS would be a rod setup of UL or L and Power BFS would be ML and up! Where does that leave us with things like a 1g trout magnet and lighter? Will we see an Extra UL (EUL) BFS category in future?

There is so much you can do with Power BFS. For me, I like to throw micro frogs for snakeheads on 15lb braided line. Yes that is thick for BFS, but it's what I do!!! I also tie a thicker leader line (or double up the line) so those snakeheads don't cut my line off. I recently did a video on Power BFS fishing for snakeheads using micro topwater frogs! (**Author's note:** *You can see this video as part of Jimmy's contributions to the supporting video media for this book*).

Other than frogging, you can also do skipping, flipping and pitching small jigs using Power BFS setup to fish cover for your favorite predatory fish.

Power BFS is a great way to throw standard size Ned Rigs. Most American anglers would use a spinning setup. I use a ML or M power rod (Moderate Fast to Fast tip) spooled with 10lb braided line and put some leader material before tying on your favorite Ned Jig. If you love the ned rig, you have to try it via Power BFS. In addition, I suggest using the Jika rig for Power BFS! You can use just about any finesse plastics you like, especially ones that are buoyant! In fact, I think the Jika Rig (Jig Rig) is even better than any Ned Jigheads out there. It casts further, more accurately and has more action!

When and why did you start your YouTube channel - and what type of content do you feature?

Oh Gosh.. hmm.. the first clip shared on YT was June 2011. I got my first GoPro and was just recording random stuff including fishing. I didn't like it at all since the quality of footage was crappie (pun intended) and my computer sucked for video editing! But so far my channel is all about fishing only. Much of it is showcasing my fishing adventures. I first started doing it to share catches with my siblings as I moved away.

As the technology of action cameras has gotten better, so has the quality of my videos! The number of subscribers grew and so I have continued to improve on my video structure and editing skills.

The type of videos I portray on my channel are mainly fishing adventures, but they always involve me showcasing either some sort of tackle or technique. Other videos I create are lure making tutorials, product reviews (such as BFS reels) and cast testing videos (which is REALLY in high demand for testing all these BFS Reels). Fishing knots seem played out, but I will make some during some of the slower seasons for indoor recording. The life of a content creator! Have to keep that ad revenue rolling!

I am hoping to add more types of content to my channel soon related to fishing and perhaps even some tips on how to grow your fishing page on Instagram!

If you had to choose a favourite fishing trip that you filmed for your channel – which would it be (and why)?

My most recent trip with my two brothers! We floated down a stream we fished when we were younger and we did it via BFS Style. Being married and away for so many years, I feel that any time spent with my siblings is a good time! But this one was special. As mentioned before, when I moved as a young teen to Delaware, my siblings were all I had until we started to fit in. So we spent time at the local creek hopping rocks, flipping rocks for critters and of course fishing! The trip was not what I had anticipated but it was the fun I have looked for. It was a fishing trip that I wanted to cross off for about 10 years! Even though this could have easily been planned and done earlier... we all just got caught up in life. Feel free to check that video episode out! Definitely was a great adventure and I recommend all to give it a try!

(Author's note: *Check out this video in the supporting video media for the book too*).

There's a big international community who target snakehead on BFS around the world; can you tell me about your power BFS approach to snakehead – including favourite rigs, rods, reels and lures please?

In North America, there are 3 species of snakeheads. The one that I target and fish in my local waters is the Northern Snakehead (*Channa argus*). This species is the 2nd largest out of all the known snakeheads. With that said, If I want to land some of these fish, I need to have the right gear.

Photo: Jimmy Ly

I often fish for snakeheads in heavy cover, so most of my gear is not BFS. Instead it's mainly a fast tip, heavy action rod as some of these fish can easily be over 8 lbs. Pulling these fish out of thick cover is no easy job! Not to mention, their bite force is insane. Hooking a snakehead is very difficult and if you have thin hooks, be prepared to lose fish as the hooks will be bent out! So why Power BFS? The challenge and it's fun! The fight is amazing and super insane on the kayak!

The spring and fall are usually great for Power BFS as there is less vegetation and you can catch them in open water. I have caught more fish using small lures than big lures. So that is why Power BFS is part of my arsenal.

My setup is very simple!

You pick your favorite BFS reel (I have so many) and pair it up with a ML Rod at least 6.5ft with a fast tip. My last setup portrayed in the snakehead video included in this book's accompanying video material was as follows - **Reel:** *KastKing Zephyr BFS*, **Line:** *Yo-Zuri Super Braid 15 lbs* , **Rod:** *KastKing Perigee II ML 6'7" Fast Tip Lure Rating 1/8th to 3/8th oz*

(Note I tied on a leader, same line, but I doubled it up. I took 3 feet of line, folded it in half and tied the Albright Knot to my main line. When completed, you now have two even leader lines, which you would use both to tie onto your lure. Alternative would be to carry at least 30lb braided line to tie on. If you don't have extra lines for the leader, you can always do a Bimini Twist to double up the line, but this method will deplete your line if you change lures often!)

Lures:
Hollow Body Frogs 3.5 Grams and up. I am very Asia-influenced when it comes to frogs. I don't like silicone legs as it causes you to lose accuracy and distance when casting. I like frogs weighted at the end as it casts further as well as it dangles rather than sit horizontal on the water.

In SE Asia, there are frogs made of wood called Jump Frogs. These guys dangle at an angle and entice fish to bite where the hook is at rather than a random spot on a frog. Japan/China loved the idea and made hollow body frog versions in many different forms. I like the ones with blades at the end as it can either buzz or you can just twitch and it will dangle the blade sub surface, hypnotising them snakeheads (even Bass) to bite! A cool small frog to look into is the one Bait Finesse Empire sells (A generic China frog) or a fancy Drave Poke Frog made and sold in South East Asia!

Soft plastics such as soft paddle tail swimbaits, fluke style lures and craws. You can often rig these on texas rig style hooks so it can be weedless or Jigs (weedless or open jigs depending water). Cheap and effective, but use thick and strong hooks! I often use Gamakatsu Superline hooks size 2/0 and 3/0.

I often like Z-man if I want to fish topwater or higher in the water column as they are buoyant. If I need to be subsurface, fishing plastics weightless on a weedless style plastic worm hook is great! Chatterbaits (Bladed swim jigs) are also great lures you can use in conjunction of your favorite plastics, but do remember to change to a heavier clip if you use Zman products. Their smaller finesse jigs sport a thinner wire clip on the blade.

In-Line Spinner Rig - I haven't seen many companies make these, but a few years back, I started making a few and sharing them on social media.

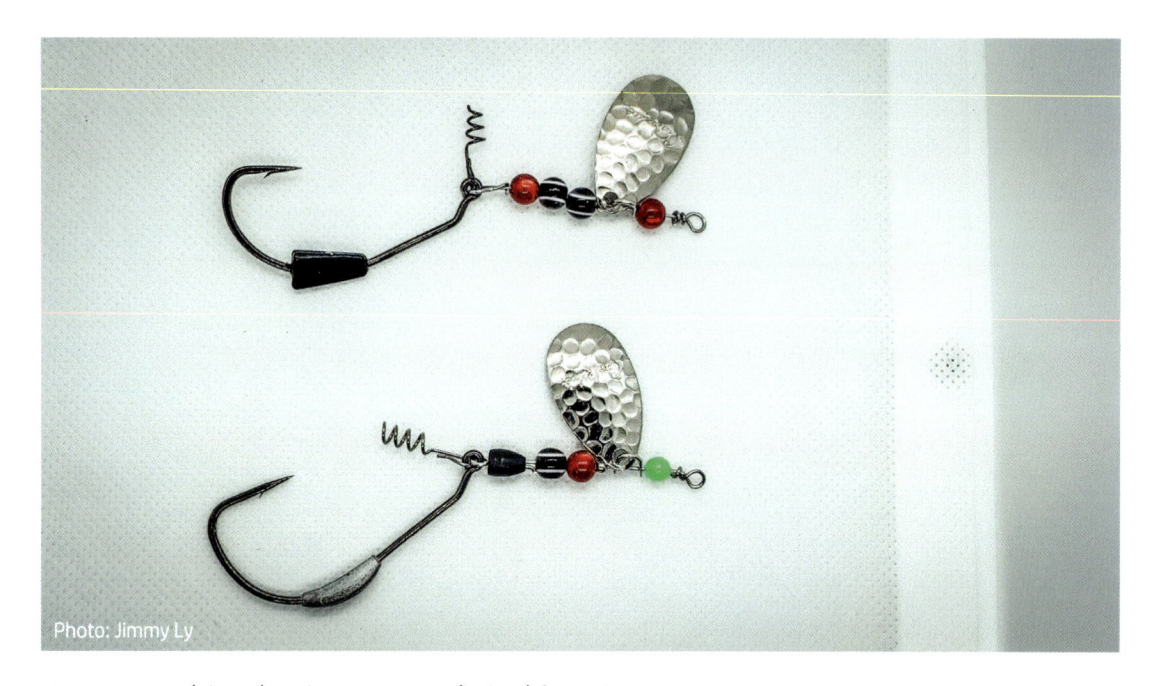

Bare mounts (above) and components (below) for In-line spinner rigging

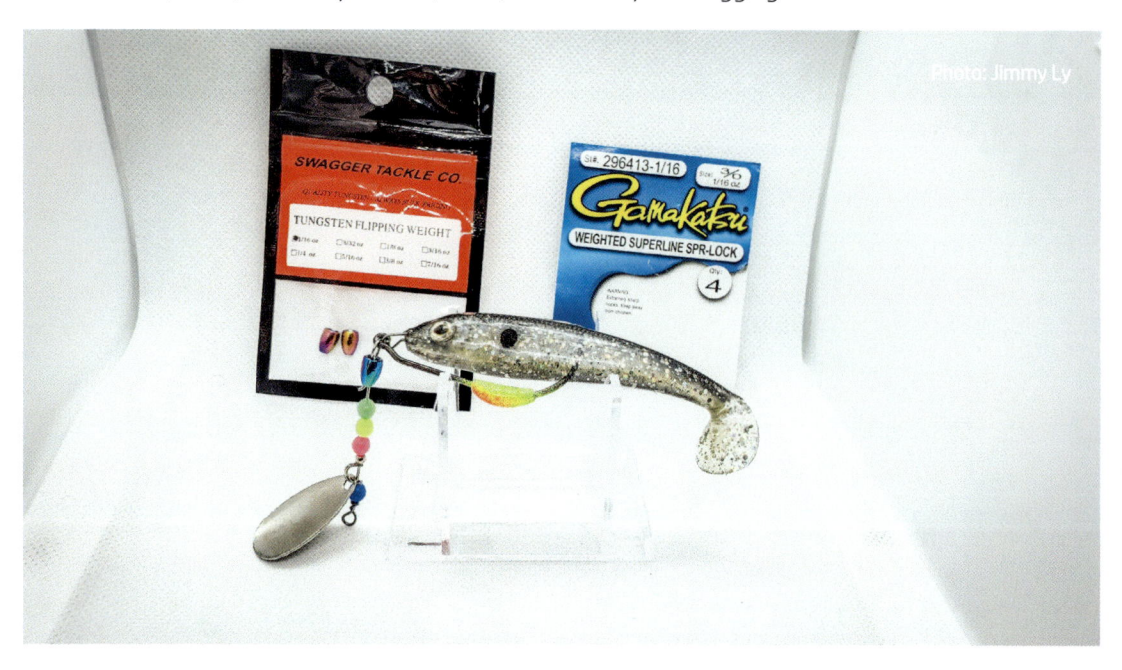

It is now one of the top lures people use to catch snakeheads and ton of custom makers in the US are making them to sell within the community! Rig them with soft plastic swimbaits and cover water!

Check the photo out, it's easy to make, but make sure you use thick wire for snakeheads! TIP: Use swimbait hooks with a screw lock and a hook weight so that it prevents line twists. Some paddle tails can generate some crazy kicks and it might cause your rig to spin.

Photo: Jimmy Ly

#thefishdontwait

Jimmy Ly

BFS Ancestory? This tubular metal **Pflueger Acehi** baitcasting rod and **Pflueger Summit 1993L** reel came from items my dad rescued from my Grandfather's house after he died in the early 1980s. They were part of a pile of stock from the fishing shop my Grandad owned in the decade leading up to World War II. The "L" in the reel model number indicates that this was the "Light Spool" model of the Summit Reel. So it seems to share the BFS ethos.

Restoring the reel let this American Bass outfit ride again in search of English pike – and I hope would make my grandad smile

Pike Between the Rain Clouds

It battered down with rain every day this week.

The rivers are all brown froth, some are bursting their banks and the the skies are a depressing grey. I haven't fished in a while and the cabin fever is definitely setting in. The weather forecast says that it *might* not rain for three hours after lunchtime today. Trouble is, where can I get to within half an hour where there is even a tiny chance I can find a feeding fish? Bait fishing is out since I don't have any bait and there's not enough time to buy some in, get to a fishing spot, set up, fish and then be back in time to sort an evening meal for the kids.

Normally this routine ends one of two ways. Either I talk myself out of even trying and end up staring impotently out through a rain-spattered window. Alternatively, I go out on some wild goose chase with too little time to fish properly (and find the fish totally dormant anyway). Against all sensible judgements I think "*What if I can find a section of canal that isn't next to farmland and might, possibly have avoided the worst of the soil runoff?*".

I know an industrial section that I can drive to in about twenty minutes - and this could fit the bill. Sod it, a 20lb wire trace plus 12lb braid was already fitted to an Aliexpress rod/reel combo (Kingdom King Pro rod with the 2-12g tip and a GH100 reel). Chucking that in the car along with my lure fishing bag and a pike net and I'm off. It stopped raining about an hour before I found somewhere to park near the footpath down the steep bank. Sling pack on my back and the net clipped onto the waist strap, I hurry down onto the towpath, put up the rod and clip a 5-g jig head hook onto the trace before adding a white and red spiky shad soft plastic swimbait (by Fox Rage).

Within half an hour the rod is arched over and a jack pike is rolling into the mesh of the net - ready to be lifted out onto the unhooking mat. Wetting the mat with the bottom of the net is an easy and instant way to protect the fish. While I didn't escape the rain (as you can see on the reel and the mat above), it felt really good to have the soft paddle-tail slammed by a couple of fish which peeled drag on a finesse outfit before high-tailing it back to the house and domestic duties.

One fish hit as the lure began to loop downwards just on the pause between cranking (I like an extended "m" shaped lure path with jig heads). The other simply smashed it on a medium-slow continuous roll. Result.

Malaysian Fish & Fishing with Christopher Lee Lian Li

Kuala Lumpur, Malaysia

Photo: Christopher Lee Lian Li

Christopher here. Born in September of 1961. Yep, 60 this year.

Grew up in a entrepreneurial and political family. My late grandfather was a founding member of the political party that got independence from the British in 1957. He was in the first parliament as MP and state assemblyman for our town.

I have been fishing and hunting since I was like 5 years old. So you could say that I have been fishing for a good 55 years. My late dad will pull me along for his hunting, fishing and aquarium fish foraging and visits to the Malaysian National Zoo, which he was a founding member. Plus he was also the founder of the Selangor Tropical Fish Association. So I guess that is why I am so interested in fishes and animals. Having grown up with fishes and wildlife.

The two men who were my mentors in fishing definitely was my father and his best friend Uncle Abu Hassan, (who went on to become a federal minister, Selangor State Chief Minister and a close golfing buddy of mine). They taught me how to fish the palm oil estate canals for Snakeheads, Tilapias and Climbing Perch.

My dad will pull me along to go search for aquarium fishes for his associations fish expos and identification of fishes in our local streams, canals, rivers, estuaries and sea.

So, you can say that I have been fishing almost my entire life.

I sort of discovered "BFS" fishing in the 80's. We did not have any dedicated BFS equipment then, but there was plenty of Ultralight Baitcasting and spinning gear around.

My fishing buddies and I got a little tired of conventional fishing so we decided to go light. With tiny fishing equipment and very light lines. As we were not catching bigger fishes. So we tried to have fun catching smaller fishes with ultralight gears. Once in a while, a giant comes by to give me a heart attack on 4lb line.

I bought baitcasting reels like the Daiwa PR10G, The Abu Garcia Ambassadeur 2500C, spinning reels like the Daiwa EL500H, Penn 712Z and 714Z. Japanese reels like The Diamond Mi-Con (Makers of the Shakespeare Sigma reels).

Snaps from Chris's personal photo album - showing a colourful and really interesting family history of politics and business!

Photos: Christopher Lee Lian Li

My fishing buddies and I will spool these UL reels with 1 to 6lb line and with modified spinning rods converted into UL BC rods we went on catch our usual prey... The Snakeheads, Tengas, a similar species of fish from the Mahseer family (*Neolisochillus hexagonolepis*) and Hampala Barbs aka Sebarau (*Hampala macrolepidota*) in our mountain streams, creeks and rivers. They were fun. I then started using lighter and lighter lines on my conventional reels. And I caught one of of my PB Barramundi (*Lates calcarifer*) of 11.75kg on my Calcutta 200CT spooled with 12lb Co-polymer line.

After that, I started using fly fishing more and more as it was the ultimate thrill on light line tippet. Plus the fly as an artificial lure... That time, I organised the first fly fishing fishing tournament in Malaysia and the whole of Asia in 1996. We had entries from Germany, Canada, Singapore, Malaysia and an audience made up of many nationalities. I got mentioned in 2 fishing magazines as the organiser of the Fly Fishing tournament. A German fly fishing magazine and a local fishing magazine who was also a prize sponsor for the winners.

I discovered BFS fishing sometime around 2011, while reading a fishing magazine whilst travelling around Asia. I was then working for HP in Boston, USA. I was managing the Asian regional big data analytics division. But due to work constraints, I could not fish much as I was travelling every week to destinations around Asia. I left HP in 2013 and went back to the airport work for Tech startups...

I then rediscovered BFS sometime in 2018, and it rekindled my interest in fishing.... I started researching more and more about BFS and SFS and started my reel collections. I started paring my reels in 2020 when the pandemic hit. Started fishing BFS seriously then.

As to the **fishes Malaysian BFS anglers and I target** these include Tarpon (*Megalops cyprinoides*), Barramundi, Giant Snakeheads (*Channa micropletes*) , The Common Snakehead (*Channa striata*) and The Bujok (*Channa lucius*) in swamps, ponds, lakes, streams, creeks and Estate canals.

The other fishes that they they and I target in the **fast flowing mountain rivers** are the Sikang (*Raiamas guttatus*) aka Malayan or Burmese Trout, the Copper Mahseer or locally known as Tengas (*Neolissochilus soroides*) , Malayan Mahseer (*Tor tamboides*) as well as the Sebarau/Hampala Barbs already mentioned.

Photos: Christopher Lee Lian Li

Then there are the **invasive species** like the Peacock Bass (*Chicla ocelaris*) , Tilapia (*Oreochromosis mosssamnbicus*) , Largemouth Bass (*Micropetrus salmoides*) , Red Tailed Catfish (*Phractocephalus hemioliopterus*) and others.

As to **my usual target species on BFS gear**, I go for The Common Snakehead, Tilapia and the Peacock Bass, Mayan Cichlid or Jaguar Cichlids (*Parachromis managuensis*) around where I live. I have to travel a distance for Barramundi and Tarpon as they are found in brackish and estuaries.

My favourite rig(s) include my Shimano Calcutta Conquest CQ HG Right hand crank with 6lb Maxima mono on a Rapala Ceratina BFS rod, My other CQ BFS HG Right Hand crank with 6lb Kastking Fluorocarbon on my Kuying Teton TTC 662L , My Daiwa Alphas Air Stream Custom 7.2 R with 2lb Maxima on my Kuying Teton TTC 510S Limited Edition and my Aldebaran BFS 6.5 with Kastking Fluorokote 4lb on my Fenwick Eagle GT UL 4-10lb. My favourite lures are the Rapala Fat Raps and the Rapala Jointed floating.

I have a small collection of other BFS reels which includes another Aldebaran BFS XG, Daiwa Alphas Air Stream Custom 7.2 R and budget reels like the the Kastking Zephyr, Royal Legend 2 (I added a BFS spool) Kyorim Black Knight BFS, Kastking Valiant Eagle BFS and Black Knight BFS 2.

Photo: Christopher Lee Lian Li

I also use my Abu Garcia Ambassadeur 2500C (this is my first UL baitcasting reel and has been by my side for over 36 years) and a local brand of baitcasting reel called a Seahawk Bass-Lite an ultralight reel that can chuck a 3g lure (this reel is also used by Abu Garcia as the AeroMax Ultralight).

One of my favourite fish to target is the Sebarau (Hampala Barb). We nick named it the Wolf of the rivers. They can grow up to 10 kgs or more, but where most of us fish they range between 800g to about 3kg... with most fish lying in the 800-g to 1.5-kg range.

What I like about catching them is their attack on the bait. They like spoons (Abu Island is a firm favourite) spinners, spinner baits and slim crank baits.   The take is savage, and I have had my gear almost ripped out of my hands by a 2-kg fella. Pound for pound they fight better than any trout. They love fast water, and usually ambush their prey in eddies and deep pockets in fast flowing streams.

My favourite retrieve methods for this fish is to use a sinking crank bait like a 7cm Rapala CD with single hooks, cast into the white waters of water falls, eddies, swirls in the streams and crank with a fast / pause / fast / pause method. They will hit it with full force. The other method I like to use is the Tokyo rig. I use a 2 inch Chartreuse or Pink paddle tail and fish it very gently. Let it sink to the bottom and give it very tiny twitches, then move it gently for about 1 crank of your reel and twitch the jig... And wait for the hit. Awesome.

 My most expensive BFS reel(s) that I own is the Calcutta Conquest BFS HG Right (I have 2 of them) My Aldebaran BFS XG and HG and My Scorpion BFS HG and 2 Daiwa Alphas Air Stream Custom 7.2 R. My budget BFS Reels are The Kastking Zephyr, Valiant Eagle BFS, Royal Legend 2 and 2 Kyorim Black Knight BFS V1 and V2.

I guess my rediscovering BFS style has made me put away my fly fishing gears. But I still tie flies to use as my BFS lures - especially for Tarpon and Peacock Bass.

Tight Lines everyone.

Chris.

Brook Trout, Trout, Panfish & Bass with Hobie-Wan Kenobi

Insta: @hobie_wan_kenobi_fishing

YouTube: Hobie-Wan Kenobi

Age: 31 Based in Michigan, USA I have been fishing for almost my whole life. I pushed fishing aside for a few years when I was really getting into sports. When I was 20, I began getting back hardcore into fishing and haven't stopped since.

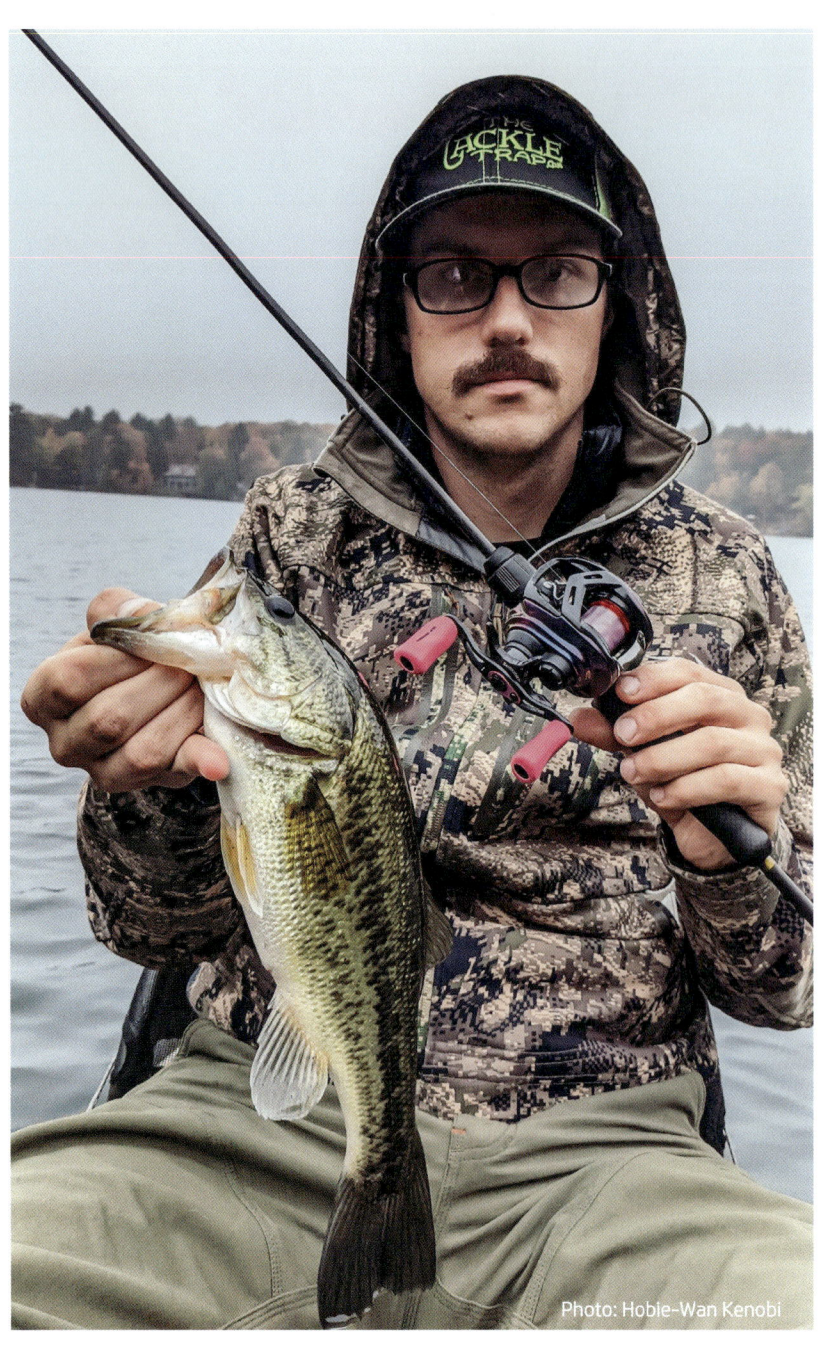

Photo: Hobie-Wan Kenobi

How long have you been fishing in general and when/how did you discover BFS?

I love ultralight fishing and I was just getting started in baitcasting reels. In 2011, I thought it would be awesome if I could combine the two styles of fishing. I was doing some research online and I came across many forum posts on the TackleTour forums about something called BFS. I tried a few different approaches and I think the BFS sickness started when I had a local rod builder build me a BFS rod with components I purchased. I remember casting a Rapala XR06 with that rod and a Daiwa PX Type-R with pure joy. I caught a small pike and I remember getting jittery with how fun it was catching a fish on ultralight baitcasting gear. That of course evolved into stream fishing for trout with BFS gear. I now make BFS content so I can help others experience that joy I have. "

What are the main species you target on BFS?

I primarily target trout and panfish with BFS gear. I also target larger species but, use BFS gear for them when the situation would usually call for spinning gear such as lightweight plastics like a shakeyhead or Ned Rig. This may clear things up, I haven't used a spinning reel since 2015 (and that was a dropshot rod)

Tell me about your favourite brook trout rod, reel, line, bait combo please!

For fishing brook trout, I believe having equipment that casts with minimal force is key to being accurate in small streams. The rod should load with minimal effort with whatever lure you are using. Brook Trout are a smaller species of trout and most that I come across are under 30cm. They get bigger than that but, I would rather be underpowered for a few fish than overpowered for most fish.

For the reel, having a lightweight shallow spool will reduce the total weight of the spool. Micro bearings also help with reducing the inertia for the cast. I have used many aftermarket spools and I have been liking the spools and bearings from Roro Lure. They are affordable and perform well above their price point.

Reel: Daiwa Alphas AIR TW 8.6L (with Roro AX24 BFS spool, standard brake)

Rod: I have a line of custom glass BFS rods that I have been working on. It is UL in power and has a very fast recovery for a glass rod. The rod loads with little force, which allows me to be very accurate as short and long range. There will be limited release of the rod to test the market and further production is a great possibility.

Line: VARIVAS Super Trout Advance Bush Trail 4lb.

Bush Trail has been great around rocks, logs and other areas that damage thin fishing line. Bush Trail has an abrasion resistant coating that I feel has allowed me to fish in abrasive areas with more confidence. I also like the orange colour, as it blends in pretty well into many of the tannic rivers I fish while still being very visible above the water.

Photo: Hobie-Wan Kenobi

What kind of baits, casting techniques (and associated rod actions) do you like for brook trout BFS?

I prefer minnow style lures for brook trout. Their aggressive nature allows for me to fish fast in stream and take advantage of their strong predatory instincts. I switch treble hooks out for single hooks to protect the fish and to also come through cover easier. Minnow style lures with single hooks are surprisingly snag resistant and allow me to fish areas that most other anglers are afraid to cast. Below are some lures I have been using this year:

Rapala Countdown CD01 (sinking)

Creep AIM 46s (sinking)

Duel Hardcore 50F Bass Minnow (floating)

Rapala Ultralight Minnow 04 (very slow sinking)

I use other lures and I am always testing new lures out and sharing my results on YouTube and Instagram.

Photo: Hobie-Wan Kenobi

An ultralight rod that loads easily with 2g is my preference. The ability to load easily with your target lure weight is crucial for accuracy and presentation. Of course, the reel having the same ability is a must as well. If you force load the rod or have to force the reel to cast your target weight, accuracy will suffer.

I like a soft yet responsive rod for twitching minnow style lures. For a production rod, I really like the Tsurinoya Ares 4'7". I have spent a few months creating a variety of prototype glass BFS rods to capture my brook trout and also some modest brown trout or rainbow fishing.

I believe that rod (**below**) is as close to small waters trout nirvana as I can reach. Responsive yet buttery smooth when hooked up. It also cushions the fight enough to keep feisty brook trout from throwing the hooks when fighting in fast current.

My most used casting technique would have to be the backhand flip as I call it. It allows the lure to be as close to me as possible, reducing the chances of the lure snagging brush on the back cast. It also requires little movement so; it reduces variables that can lead to inconsistent casting. It does require a deeper flexing rod to be effective. If I am using a faster action rod, I use a backhand roll cast.

What sort of venues do you fish for smallmouth bass in and, when you're not deep-cranking on heavier gear; what does your favourite BFS outfit look like for smallies?

River dwelling smallmouth and ones that live in lakes are similar and so different at the same time. I tend to power fish with big crankbaits, topwater, spinnerbaits and other lures for lake smallmouth.

When fishing streams that hold smallmouth, I prefer to use the same approach as I do for trout. Smallmouth tend to prefer slower water than the trout but, are often caught in the same areas.

Catching smallmouth on trout BFS gear gives me an anxious feeling of joy when I am hooked up. They fight so hard and do everything from launching out of the water to digging into the nearest log to get unhooked.

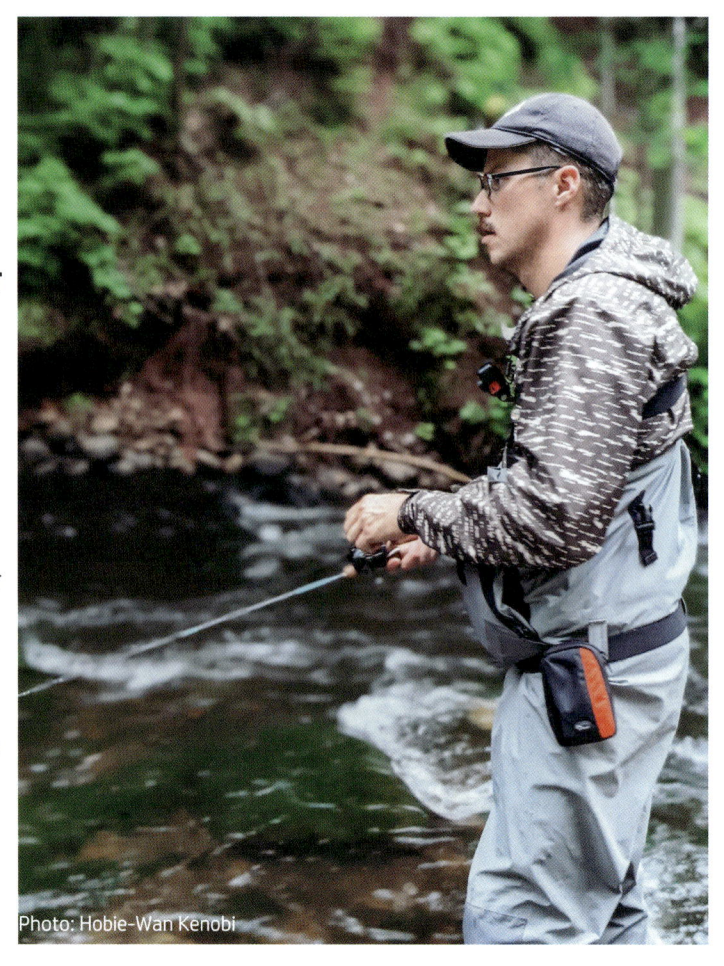

Photo: Hobie-Wan Kenobi

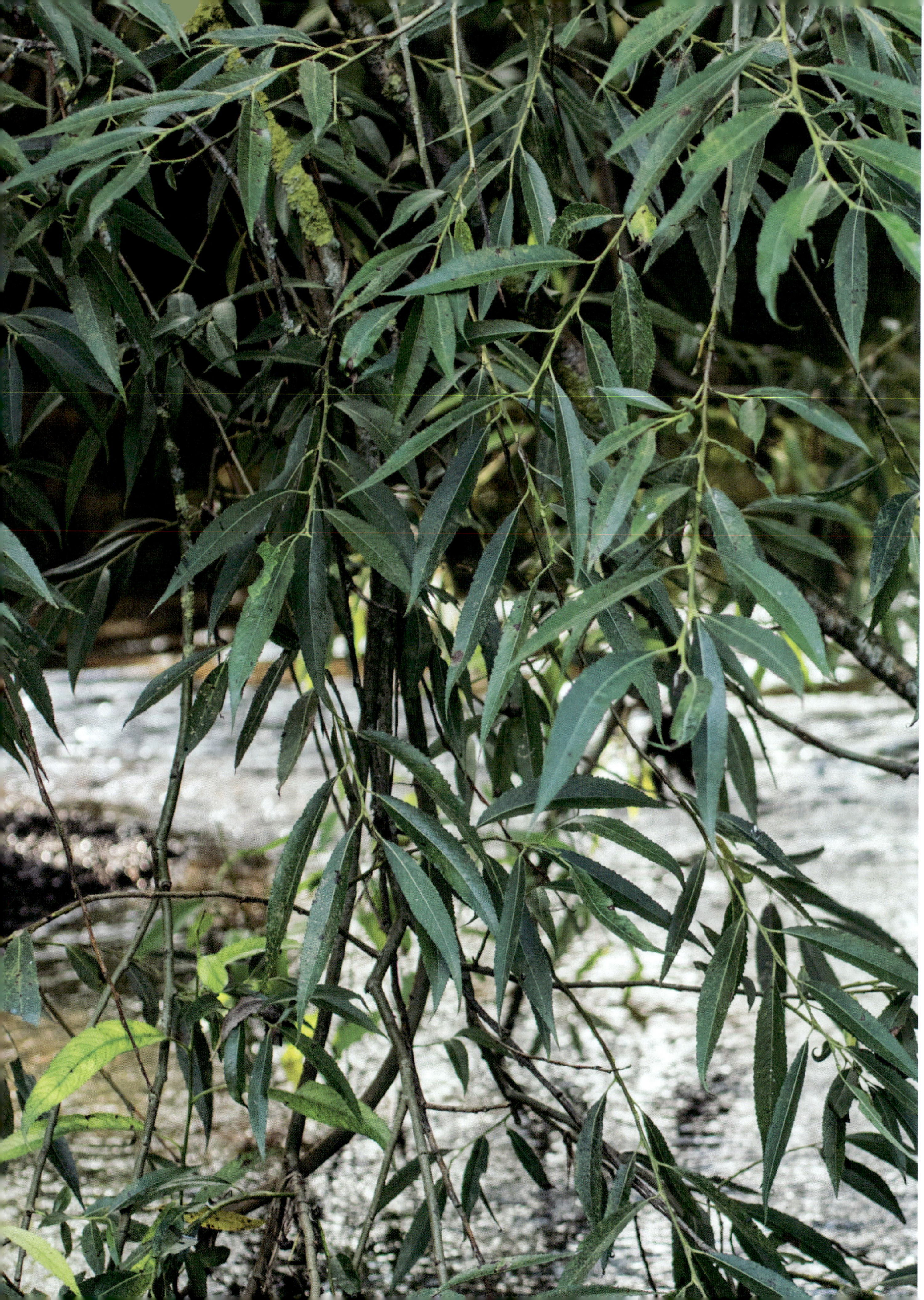

Secret Creek

I fished a new stream with a Zoner Minnow & a glass rod

This is the story that set the ball rolling for this book project. It was something shared with everyone who had subscribed to the BFS VIPs newsletter via the Fishing Discoveries website. The response it got was really very surprising - with so many people emailing to say that they loved it. From there it seemed like there was room to create a book around inspiring new adventures for anyone interested in being part of the BFS "Tribe".

The photos in the story are just snaps from my phone - since this was an honest to god escape from the working day. I just grabbed my fishing gear and left with no thought of recording anything for anyone except myself. Selfish but also true. Anyway, read on over the page to find out how this went down.

As I write this I'm still buzzing from a stolen few hours of fishing yesterday evening (amazing how "fishing therapy" benefits stay with you).

I'd had more than enough of work, and I needed to escape before I lost the plot; but I didn't have much time.

One of the cool things about fishing short, ultralight rods with lures is that they can turn even the most humble water into a potential adventure. A fresh challenge was an exciting prospect - and I even felt like it wouldn't matter if I made more than a handful of casts. It just seemed important to be outdoors and around water.

After finding a new blue line within striking distance on Google maps, I was soon parked up and bushwhacking towards a small channel in the cooling evening air.

Oh, and because this was "me time" - I didn't pack the heavy camera gear, tripod, waterproof backpack and all the rest of my usual blogging kit. I just had my beat-up phone to take some snaps if anything interesting happened...

So it was that I found myself under a very scruffy (and graffiti-covered) concrete bridge and banks infested with invasive Himalayan balsam - hardly a glamorous spot!

But, there was flowing water - so perhaps (if it had avoided pollution) there could be fish hiding nearby? It didn't look as if people fished here and the access wasn't so easy.

Maybe that was because it isn't worth bothering?

...the nagging doubt that also adds spice to tackling a water "on sight" with zero prior knowledge.

As with all adventures, little rituals are important to give them a sense of occasion. The idea of carefully unpacking a little leather "treasure box" containing my re-furbed Ambassadeur reel and fancy aluminium rod-tube strapped to my pack with a lovely custom-build glass rod made me grin in these untidy, unloved surroundings:

With low water and a need for stealth, I decided to tie on a 50-mm (2") Zoner. At 1.7g, it makes very little splash even when landing on flat water; as long as you can set it down reasonably gently at the end of the cast.

A handful of downstream casts into a very fishy looking spot below the bridge and nothing to show for it allowed some doubts to creep in. Just as I was halfway through my last cast before leaving that spot, a sharp tug on the line showed that there was indeed life in this stream.

A few extra casts for good luck - and no more action - but now I was smiling and happy that I at least had a chance here.

I turned upstream, above the bridge and cast into shallow water (the sort of spot where predators might herd minnows up against the shore). Third cast in - I miss another hard pull; then success! I'm attached to a jagging, fussing, spiky little perch as it splashes all the way to the net.

At this, I am indescribably happy. Never mind the size of this fish; it is absolutely beautiful and it felt great on the ultralight 1 to 5-g blank. Plus, it materialised from a piece of water that was a total "black box" quantity; which is so close to the pure childhood experience of fishing.

Another perch follows soon after and I miss a couple of chances before moving upstream into a pinch-point that is significantly deeper (with a soft, clay bottom along with some more reassuring gravel underfoot in places).

Here I miss another tug - before a tiny chub obliges and stays attached long enough for a photo.

Now a slightly larger chub joins the party - and this seems to be a fun summer venue for small coarse fish (perhaps affected by intermittent pollution which might keep the fish small - and keep the trout away?).

Then, I'm working up against a bank where two separate foam lines from a riffle upstream join together and wham, I'm attached to another small chub taken from calf-deep water. Or so I think. The "chub" jumps and fizzes its tail against the surface - revealing itself to be a small (and lovely) trout!!

My idea of what this place is - and what it might offer were instantly exploded by the little fish below. Now I knew that it is clean enough to support adult trout breeding efforts - and that their offspring are happy to hang around.

It also means there could be anything grabbing my lure next...Another long, relatively slow glide is ahead and I can see a pod of small chub sipping down the occasional insect (probably aphids, judging by the shower of them that fall down my neck and shower the top of my pack like fine green snow as I push through some overhanging sycamore branches).

I hook and lose several chub, land a small one and have a few more follows and another missed strike. Then it goes quiet for a while.

Soon I'm daydreaming and half-heartedly casting towards what (I lazily realise) would probably make the mother of all big-trout lies in any other river...but not this little stream of course...

Maybe the stream felt insulted by that thought? Either way, I am left slack-jawed when a near 20" trout torpedoes across the shallows swiping its head left and right trying to grab my Zoner as it runs up the edge of a small gravel beach (formed around an ancient, semi-buried car bonnet).

The fish runs out of water before it can reach my lure - and on one of its swipes, it's eyes lock with mine and the game's up as it bolts back out into its hidey hole. Busted.

It did not come back for a second look at the lure.

Now, though, all bets are off - I mentally apologise for patronising the stream and its (now terrifying) prospective inhabitants.

Not quite at sunset yet, but there is a lovely glow (and a further cooling in temperature) that I hadn't noticed until that huge trout woke me up. Into the pool above the head of the next riffle upstream and suddenly my rod is bent double, the drag is peeling out line and another big trout is thrashing on the surface. I just have time to think "wow, this is exciting - though it's not quite as big as the bruiser in the pool below" - when it spits the hook and the lure nearly takes my head off.

Again, I apologise to the fish and the stream - since I didn't mean to insult the size of the trout. I wasn't disappointed in its size, I was just making an observation OK??

No, that excuse never seems to wash when you comment on someone's fashion sense either...Go figure.

A little further upstream and there is a narrowed, deepened canyon pinched between willow bushes on my left and a vertical bank created from steel sheet-piling on the right. The piling "bank" seems to support a small business' yard some 10 to 12 feet overhead. Second cast in to the tail end of that run and the lure is thumped by something that means business. Again drag is peeling, the rod is bending mightily and a good-sized trout is sloshing left and right - sometimes on the surface, showing its brassy flank and often diving towards any available cover. This time, we stay attached long enough to share a quick photo while we both recover. By now I'm pinching myself since this is just evolving into the dream session (given the dire need for therapy matched by the sudden, unplanned adventure in a mystery stream close to home).

After this, things are a bit of a blur. I miss some more chances and notice that the light is fading. I become aware that wading back to the nearest point I can climb out of the channel could be "interesting" if it got much darker. Although the stream is small, with lots of shallow features - the bed is soft and mobile. Where it gets pinched between obstructions or hard banks - it can create drop-offs that exceed the limits of my chest waders...I'll just fish through to the head of the next riffle I tell myself. Fortunately, one more trout takes pity on me and allows me to finish on a fish, right as I get to my destination point. The photo (right) is authentically blurry because the light, by now, is really quite poor (especially under the trees).

Although a bit shorter than the previous trout, this one actually took more line as it ran straight up the pool against the flow. It has a tail on it like a Lough Corrib special and puts an absolute exclamation point on an unexpectedly wonderful, spontaneous couple of hours. I hope you don't mind me sharing this particular personal trip with you. My excuse is that it just seems to perfectly sum up the world of possible adventures that BFS fishing can open up to you. I dare say I'd never have thought to fly fish that section of stream if I didn't own a BFS or very short, ultralight lure rod - and the fact this little river was hiding in plain sight just made it magical.

I half expect, the next time I go to fish there, I'll find out it doesn't actually exist (and I'd dreamed the whole thing).

If I'm lucky though, Narnia will still be on the other side of the wardrobe when I need to decompress again.

89

Building a Bait Finesse Empire with Amir Azzabi

Insta: @baitfinesseempire

Web: https://baitfinesseempire.com/

Owner and founder of Bait Finesse Empire online BFS store: Created to spread the love of "Bait Finesse System" fishing in North America. For the glory of finesse!

Photo: Amir Azzabi

I was born and raised in Arizona, USA. 34 years later, and Arizona is still my home. Like a lot of anglers in the Western US, I grew up fishing and hunting with my family on weekend camping trips around the state. Back then the go to technique was a worm, corn, or some dough bait on an as cheap as they come spinning combo. But fishing is fishing and the joy of being outdoors and the thrill of the catch was deeply embedded into me from a young age. As a young adult I began the journey into lure fishing, and with that came countless hours of researching and testing out gear that has led me to the passion I have today.

When and how did you first get into BFS?

I first learned about Bait Finesse Fishing about 5 years ago while browsing the internet for new finesse techniques and gear. I ended up spending months just researching what was out there, how the technique was being utilized, and how it could apply to my fishing conditions and styles. Then, like all American anglers interested in bait finesse at the time, I ordered my first bait finesse gear online and had to wait about two months for it to be shipped in from overseas. My very first combo was a Kuying Teton Ultra-Light rod paired with a not-so-great CDM reel. The reel has since been worked out of my line-up, but that rod is one I still use on occasion.

What is it about this style of fishing which keeps you addicted?

I'll admit that I've got the gear monkey on my back, so it's the gear.

Finesse techniques have always been my go-to style. Long before I knew about bait finesse fishing, I was using small lures and traditional bass finesse techniques to target the highly pressured fish in my local waterways on spinning tackle. It's simply what works well here. So of course, as I learned about a whole new way to fish finesse presentations, the thought of diving into a whole new category of fishing gear was in itself a big excitement for me. Once I was able to experience first-hand the technical advantages offered by bait finesse tackle, I was completely hooked.

Which fish species have you targeted with BFS, and do you have any favourites?

I primarily target urban bass. When I'm lucky enough to find time to get out of the city I'm generally at a mountain stream chasing either rainbow trout or one of our native (Gila and Apache) trout species. While bass can offer the excitement of a big fish on light tackle, it's hard to beat the natural sceneries and technical complexities that come with mountain stream fishing.

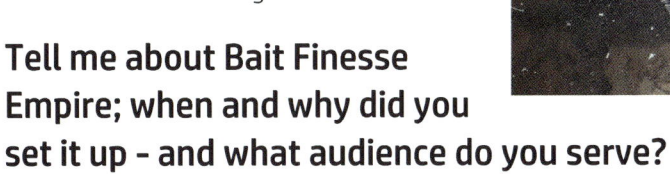

Photo: Amir Azzabi

Tell me about Bait Finesse Empire; when and why did you set it up - and what audience do you serve?

I first thought to start Bait Finesse Empire, as a way to help make bait finesse fishing more accessible to the North American angler, in January of 2021. By that point the popularity of bait finesse fishing had grown exponentially through YouTube, social media platforms, and online forums, but the specialized gear needed to fish the style was still something that was not readily available in the US. Founding Bait Finesse Empire was my way of contributing to the sport in that sense. As I began to lay the groundwork for how the business would operate, I reached out to raWr Fishing and Hobie-Wan Kenobi to "pitch" my idea and was lucky enough to receive positive responses back from both. Their honest feedback and tremendous passion for the sport was and continues to be a vital part of what makes Bait Finesse Empire work. From concept to reality only took three short months, and we were able to officially open Bait Finesse Empire to the public in April of 2021.

What kinds of lures do you tend to throw for your own fishing (and what are your "confidence" options)?

I throw all varieties of finesse lures, from spoons to topwater to jigs to minnow lures. Part of my love of the sport is the gear, the variety of options out there, and learning how to efficiently fish new lures and techniques. That said, there are two rigs that I tend always have on hand when I'm out at the local urban ponds. A dropshot with a 3-6" finesse worm and a 2" paddletail swimbait paired to a small skirted jig. When nothing else is getting bit, I can generally count on these two techniques to come through for me.

Tell me about your favourite BFS trip so far please

In early 2020 I was lucky enough to help prototype some bait finesse rods from a well-known American rod company. I methodically fished these rods for months in all my usual spots, catching all my usual fish, but knowing that my doing so and the feedback I was providing was a key part of making a true bait finesse rod a reality for the US market made the whole experience standout and memorable.

What's your favourite rod action/style and what typical ranges do you cast?

For bait finesse fishing bass my go to is a seven-foot, fast action, light power rod. The added length helps with casting further and insuring proper hooksets. Most of my go to bass lures end up being between 2.5 and 5 grams when fully rigged.

For trout bait finesse fishing in creeks, I like using rods between 5 and 6 feet with a mod-fast action. The shorter casting distances and moving water play well to the advantages of this style of rod. Most of my trout lures tend to be in the 1.5 to 4 gram range when fully rigged.

Author Note: *If you're in the North American continent and need to stock up on anything BFS-related, check out Bait Finesse Empire on the URL given in Amir's Bio at the beginning of this chapter. There's a constantly-updated selection of very cool stuff from Japan and China at a range of price-points.*

Even if you're not in the market for new lures, rods, lines reels - check out the @baitfinesseempire instagram reels, posts and stories to keep on top of latest lures that are working and also the activities of folks fishing with BFE gear across the USA. This is great for staying on top of current trends and is a valuable service to the BFS community - thanks Amir!

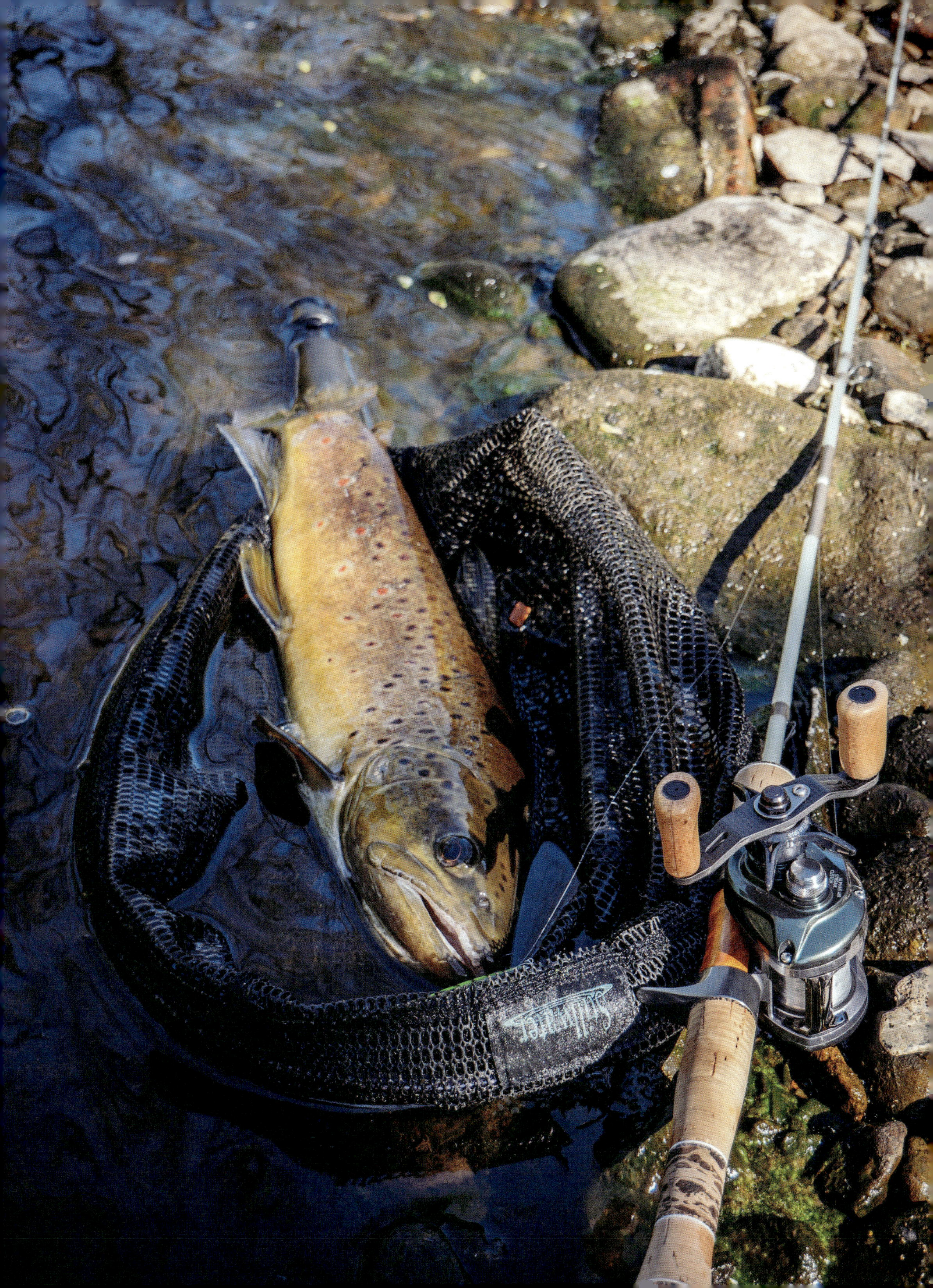

Lockdown Perch

In January 2021 we were in a COVID lockdown situation that only allowed local travel to fishing spots. The exact radius which wouldn't get you fined if you went beyond it wasn't always clear over the different stages of each lockdown. However, being able to walk to a fishing venue was definitely a safe bet.

Over a few weeks of snowfall and very few cars moving around on the roads, I came to rely on the occasional trudge through the creaky snow (or light frost, depending on the day) carrying an extendable "street fishing" net-handle and my BFS gear to get some fishing done. The extendable net can be vital in winter if you are to fish safely off some of the vertical banks above a freezing cold river. Trying to reach down one of those with a standard, short-handled net on frozen mud is a recipe for an unplanned, probably one-way trip to the bottom of the pool.

As I mentioned in the very first story in this book, my home river is often a case of feast and famine. With more people turning to fishing as a means of looking after their mental wellbeing during lockdown, lure fishing would more often lean towards the famine experience for many trips.

Couple that with cold water and feeding spells would be pretty localised and maybe also short-lived too (even without additional angling pressure). The flip side of those odds being stacked against you on many trips is that any success you did enjoy was massively magnified. Over the course of probably four of those trips where I'd tramp from my front door through the back-streets and then slip/slide my way down a wooded path to the river I caught one modestly-sized chub. That fish came just as darkness was falling in the mid/late afternoon (daylight hours are pretty short in Yorkshire during the middle of winter).

Don't get me wrong, the sense of achievement for that one lure-caught fish was really something. Sure I could probably have caught more on bait while throwing in loose feed to induce more fish to feed - but I didn't really fancy carrying tons of gear and ground bait the kind of distance I was walking. The act of being mobile with a BFS rod is also a pretty useful way of staying warm in cold weather.

Maybe there is also something in the act of many, many repeated casts while lure fishing when you are not catching that allows your mind to wander and chew through things in a healthy way. Possibly the distraction of catching fish - as wonderful as that is - may interrupt that patching up and healing process. It is said that a degree of boredom is actually necessary for good mental health. In fact, one of the biggest threats to mental health is the instant gratification offered by social media and other online resources (with app designers deliberately engineering dopamine spikes in

A trampled section of bank created a patch with just a few remnants of melting slush and snow

response to checking for interactions or approval for our posts). Another big problem is when our *expectation* of reward is greater than the reality of that reward; a terrible downward spiral which, I'm told, actually lowers your baseline dopamine levels too.

I guess that makes it easier to imagine the extreme surprise and joy when, after thousands of empty casts, changing to a heavier 5-g cheburaska weight for a floating soft stickbait results in a fish smashing the bait as soon as it hits bottom. That territorial smash alone was surprising enough - then when the hook-set is met with fierce thumping head-shakes and short frenetic runs; the realisation that this could be a big perch ramps up the excitement further.

For my little home river, the perch above is a really big fish - seeing its huge flank roll flat, beaten on the surface as I get the net down to it is an astonishing sight. Drawing it over the net rim is true heart-in-mouth stuff.

Even looking back at the photograph nearly a year later still produces butterflies in my belly. Thank you Mr Perch!

Italian Bait Finesse with Tsurikichi Nikke

*The Japanese fishing anime series **Sanpei Tsurikichi** is incredibly popular in Italy. As a result it is really common for anyone who is mad about fishing to have the nickname "Tsurikichi" ("Fisherboy" or "Fishing Enthusiast"). Nikke is a fellow tenkara addict and, when he found out I also had an interest in BFS, he very generously gave me the benefit of his experience (as he has been teaching this style of fishing for a while in his homeland of Italy)*

Nikke has kindly agreed to share his thoughts (in English) on what makes BFS so compelling for him - as well as sharing images of big chub, gear and the lovely streams he fishes.

The unbearable lightness of the ... Lure!

The title is brazenly taken from the novel by Milan Kundera but it is so suitable that I am not ashamed at all to use it!

Many fishermen have experienced the ultralight and, especially in spinning, I have had the impossible dream of being able to move my bait while avoiding the restrictions of my fishing line.

The ideal (and impossible) would be to have a lure more as if it were not attached to anything at all...Ultralight is a byword for narrow creeks, accurate casting, gentle poses and last but not least ... the art of getting by!

Even so, it seems like such a notable difficulty but the continuous search for the Zen-inspired "perfect cast", together with the modern technology, allowed me to undertake new levels of fishing with the ultralight casting, today called BFS.

What was it that allowed me to accomplish those results, I could have easily reached with a normal spinning equipment, without so many complications? The answer is: my stubborn temper with only my personal satisfaction as an alibi!

It was like reliving the period of my "fishing career", full of willingness to learn and pride in capturing fish without using natural baits.

It is exactly as the air you breathed at your first catch made with BFS.

Tsurikichi Nikke

June 2021

April Fools' Trout

In which I find myself with an afternoon free on April 1st

Although the vegetation was still quite drab and the temperature cool, I noticed that the fly hatches were underway and the trout had well and truly woken up from their winter and early spring stupor.

A cancellation of planned work left me with an entire midweek afternoon to do exactly as I pleased.

There was a spot I knew a little under an hour away that I hadn't fished for several years (and I'd always fished with either fly rod or tenkara rod before). Reports of pollution and a fish kill gave some nagging doubts – but after all, nothing ventured/nothing gained...

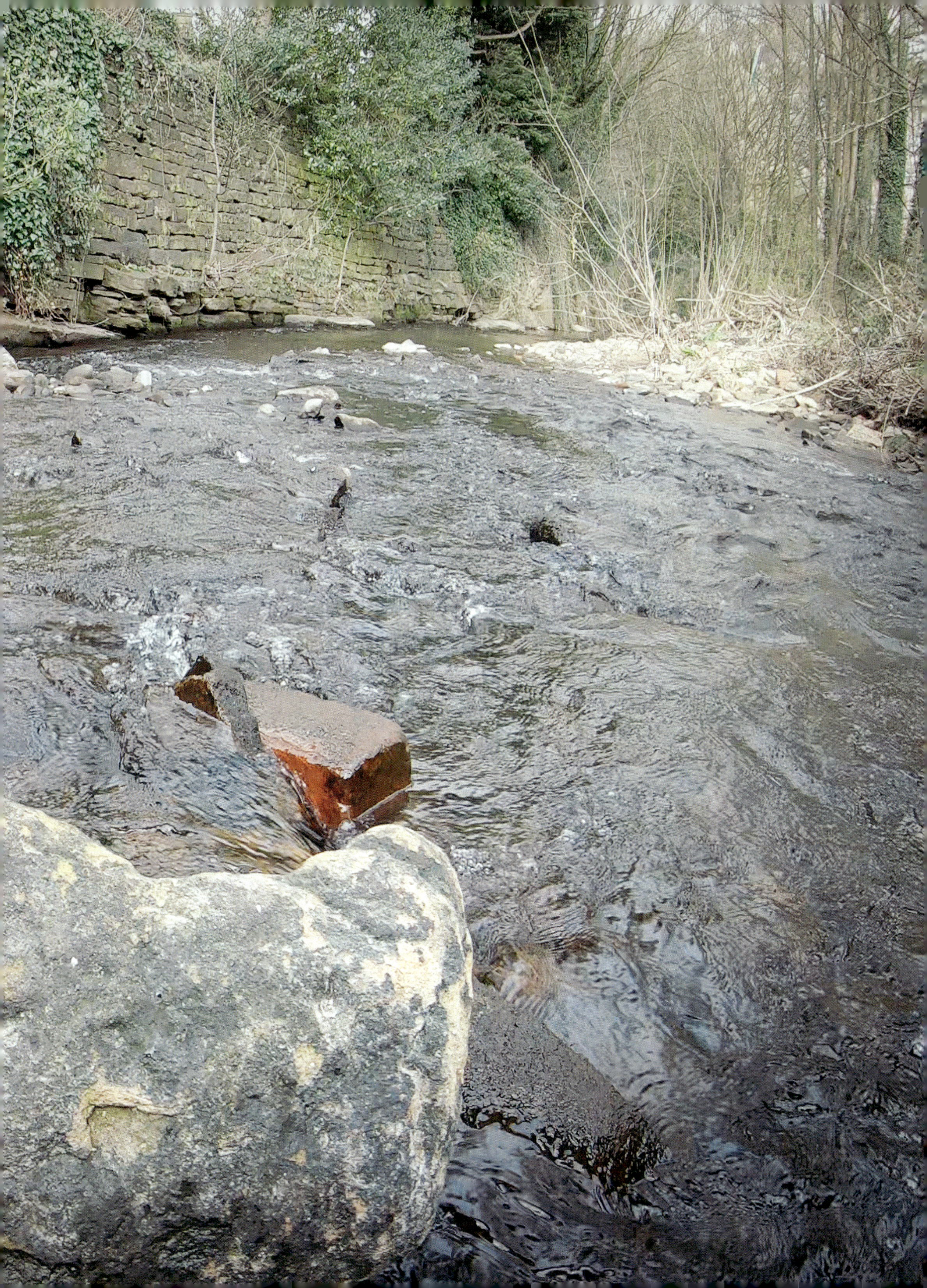

The day is a mixture of watery/misty sunshine and cloud but it feels great to be driving along the winding country lanes. Swooping down the dips (where the kids always shout "wheee" whenever they're riding in back) with the hedges and dry-stone walls blurring by on both sides. I really like this journey because it takes me through a rolling/rugged landscape while travelling at a good pace without needing to get into the monotony of motorway driving.

Even though much of the vegetation is still very drab, undeveloped and winter-like, there is a definite feeling of the spring about to happen. Occasionally the sun and a patch of blue sky breaks through for a minute or so before being swallowed up again by the light grey, smudged clouds. I packed an ultra-delicate wand today (Teton TTC 510S, 5'10" rated for lure 0.3-3g) and also the Clamber Hyper Micro HM06, spooled with 50m of 4-lb fluorocarbon. This is the first time I've been able to take this outfit fishing - and I think it should be a great match for targeting wild trout in a hillside stream.

There is a slight worry over stories of fish killed in this stream by a bad pollution event from an industrial source a couple of years ago and - even if there are any trout left - would they actually be willing to chase a lure. The river is a strange one to find. It snakes around between villages and small towns on the edge of the Pennine Chain of hills (known as the Backbone of England) - but doesn't seem to see a lot of fishing attention until the lower reaches. On the approach there is a tremendous switchback road which drops you from the valley top right down to the river level. It's a strange setting because of the history of cotton and wool mills in this part of the world - it means you get these small villages but with big, old, sandstone-walled mills and industrial premises that were at the heart of the industrial revolution. Over time, nature has reclaimed a lot of the settings where previous industries looked to harness water power - though many of the weirs are still intact and causing problems for river habitat regeneration. It isn't just the prevention of free movement of fish between the different habitats they need to complete their lifecycles, it is also the blocking of downstream transport of riverbed rocks and gravel. That turnover and resupply of the building blocks of habitat is vital for healthy rivers and everything living in them. That being said, the rivers where weirs slowly crumble and become reabsorbed into the river - and where factory walls become overgrown with ivy, ferns and moss - make for some really atmospheric settings to catch fish.

I have a favourite car park behind a shop in this village where I can do a kind of superman/phone-booth style transformation into waders. It's easy to make a temporary changing room behind the open driver's side door of a car and the sandstone wall. Using the floor mat from the car is also a good move for protecting stocking foot waders from punctures while putting on wading boots. After many years of fishing in post-industrial and full-on urban rivers, I have this routine down pretty well by now.

There are no fishing-brand or fishing-related stickers on the outside of the car or in the windows and I pretty much carry everything with me while fishing (aside from my trainers). That way there is nothing to tempt or alert any thief who might otherwise find my window worth breaking in order to find out what's under the parcel shelf. I also like to use a folding landing net (a kind of "concealed carry" arrangement) as well as rigging up on the river away from the car so as to avoid drawing attention to the vehicle and its possible contents.

A long time ago I had a pair of fly rods, several reels and fly boxes containing around 6-years worth of fly tying stolen out of the boot of my car when I had pulled up to the flat I was living in (in a "nice" part of town). I never saw any of it again and the flies took a long time to replace. The insurance excess fee on the glass breakage was expensive enough that I now usually leave my (empty) car unlocked - particularly when I'm fishing. Camera gear never leaves my side (well, my waterproof slingpack) until it is time to pop off the lens cap and shoot some photos. I sometimes wear a chest-mounted action camera too, but again that sticks to me at all times.

At least here there is a pretty affordable pay and display ticket machine along with CCTV. The fact that old stone steps in the corner of the car park lead you down to a trout stream is also a big plus in my book. A quick, purposeful walk along the wall and down the steps brings me out next to a little rain-fed river with that familiar beer/tannin stain. As always, when you're right down in the river there is a distinctive, cool dank-cave smell which you don't really experience even when on the footpath a few feet above water level.

I put up the rod, thread the guides and tie on an ayu pattern 50-mm Zoner Minnow with single hooks. A passing dog walker asks "so are there actually any fish in there mate?". My reply is an honest "I really don't know yet" and he looks at me with a slightly confused expression - perhaps mixed with a small dose of pity. While I set the brakes and the drag he continues on his way; mallard ducks on the path scooting out of reach of the dog on its lead while trying to look as if they're not hurrying. As I make my first cast I notice two swirls made by separate fish taking small insects from the surface as they hatch. That is very encouraging given the previous fish-kill. Casting into the main tongue of current coming down the centre of the pool (left) gives the minnow some disguise as it lands in the turbulent surface. Right away I miss two fish on consecutive casts! Damnit! Dropping casts into the deeper eddy formed below the collapsing wall on the left as you face upstream - the anticipation is running high.

Then, wham! A fish peels back out of the eddy and nails the minnow just as it draws into the main tongue of current on a fairly short cast. It goes airborne almost straight away and spends most of the short but spirited fight splattering around on or above the water surface. Reaching down with the net after taking it out of its holster and shaking it open, the fish skitters crazily to my left and forces me to chase it with the net to scoop it up. Success! The buttery belly and rusty-orange fins brighten up the grey, slightly misty day down in the valley bottom. With the first fish in the net, happiness floods through me. Not only because of the gamble to come here paying off, but also to see these wild trout hanging on and bouncing back - even in the face of a dose of water pollution. My guess is that at least some of these fish will have travelled downstream from above the source of the problem over the last couple of years.

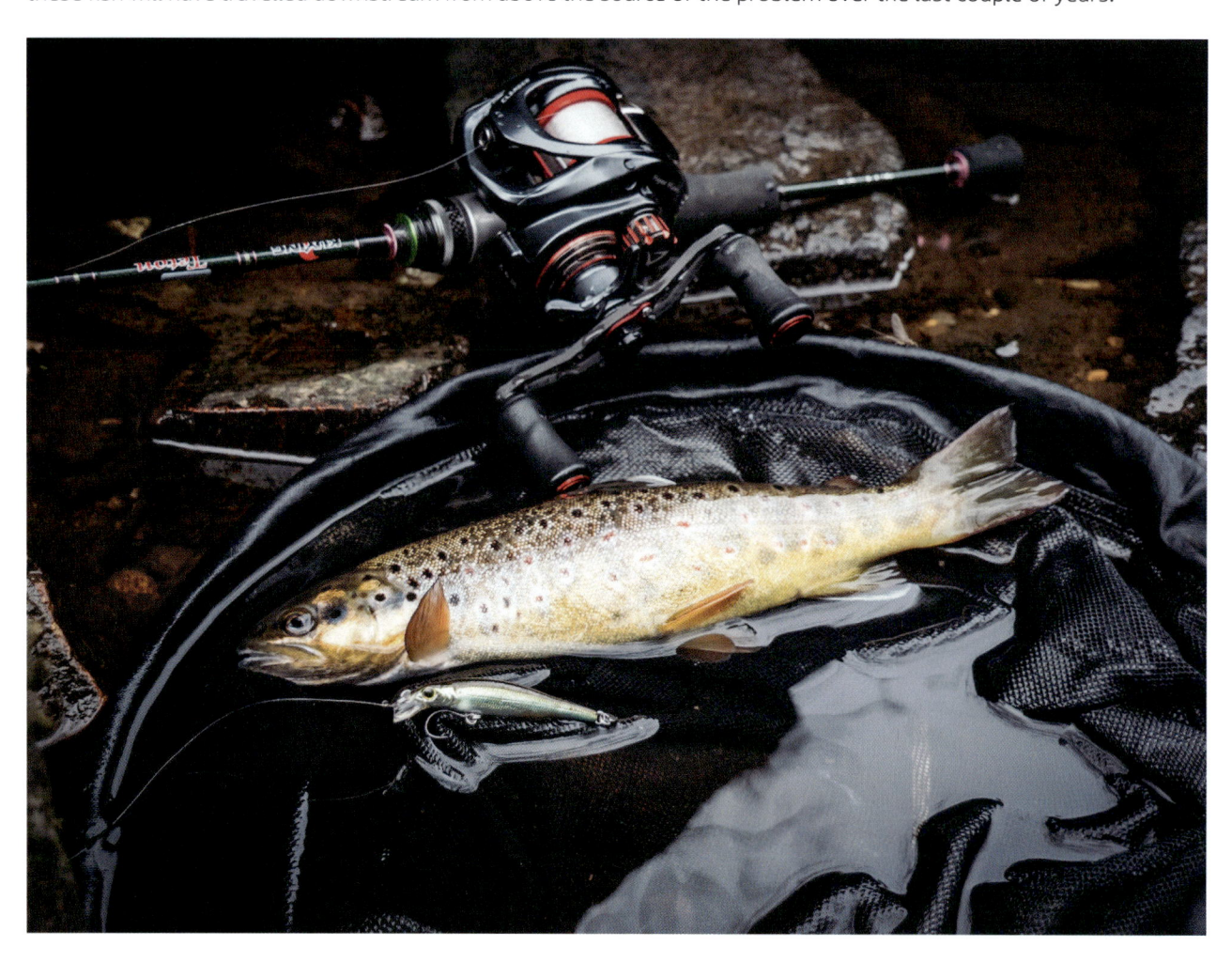

Again, the faint grey body-barring and round splodges towards the tail (aside from the red and black haloed spots) remind me of those Japanese trout - while still being unmistakably a "brownie". As I turn the fish over the rim of the net to release it, I notice the tail of a small, unfortunate, baitfish poking out of its mouth! Despite having a complete belly full, that trout certainly liked the ayu-pattern Zoner (which was perhaps even slightly smaller than its last meal).

With three fish contacted within the first two minutes confidence is sky high. Naturally, that meant the fish need to give me a slap in the face as this pool fails to produce any further action - and nothing happens in the next long run upstream either. Rounding a right-hand bend shows that crossing the river to fish from the opposite bank gives the best shot in towards the deeper central water and holding spots at the foot of a vertical stone wall. Two small fish follow and frantically harass the minnow - but neither commits to grabbing hold.

Time to move to a new spot and try to freshen things up. Another feeling I really like about exploring these post-industrial rivers is being able to go underneath road bridges and tunnels. Quite often the newer road infrastructure conceals much older bridge stonework that just isn't visible from street level. When the sunlight breaks through the clouds, it makes the water shine bright amber and shows up every feature on the riverbed too. I guess this is the half-rural version of urban exploration and you do get a strange pleasure from being in places other folks don't usually see.

Above this bridge I have a really good fish swipe at the lure - before locking eyes with me and scooting below some big sunken boulders. The deeper, rock-strewn water screams bigger fish - but I can't buy any further interest until I move up into the glide above. It is in the oily, slick flow of this glide that I hook, battle and then lose by far the biggest fish of the day. I'm absolutely gutted as the lure pings free right as the fish is at the net and it would have made a spectacular photo. However, two casts later I hook up and land another decent fish - which I'm really pleased with. I'd be lying if I said that I wasn't still disappointed to lose the bigger fish - but that's totally separate from appreciating what is a lovely trout to finish my trip on (the time bell is ringing and I need to bug out and get home to sort out the kids). While I'm photographing this last fish, the sun peeks through the clouds again for just about thirty seconds. It totally transforms the colours, texture and vibrance of the markings.

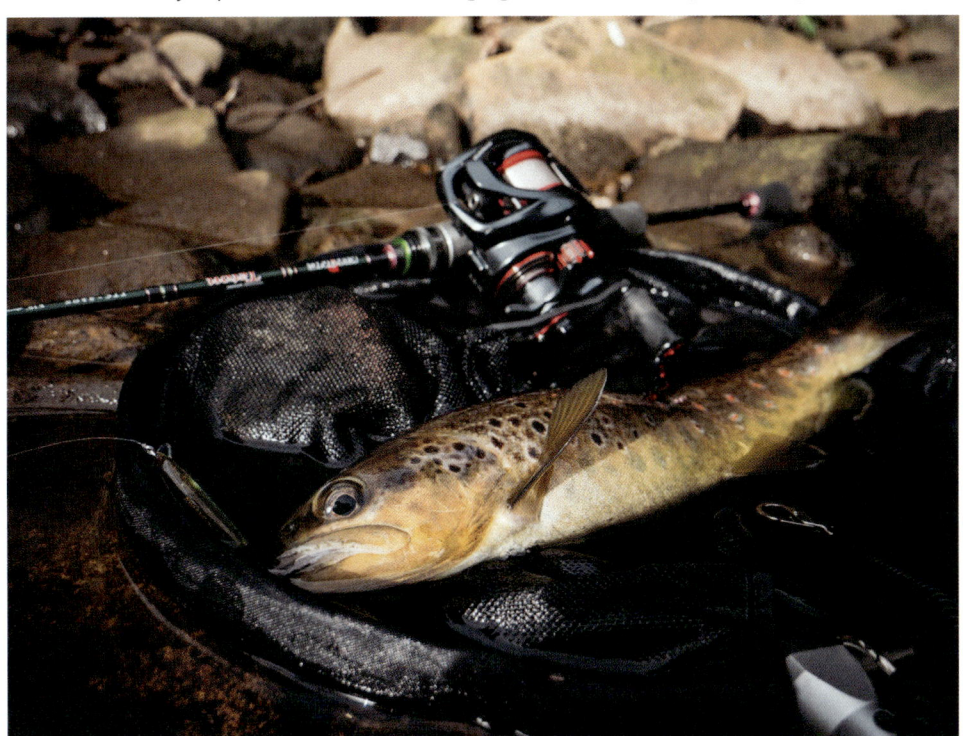

Sloshing through the shallows and tramping over cobbles to hurry back to the car gives me time to realise what a delicate and crisp combination of rod, reel and ultralight minnow I got to enjoy today.

Pulling away in the car, I can't wait to come back again - and that is always a sign of a day well-spent.

Needham's Specialist Tackle with Jamie Needham

Age: 21, Manchester UK

Currently working full time as a Cylindrical Grinding Machinist. Jamie has been fishing for around the last 7 years & lure fishing for the last 5. He also races motocross & mountain bikes at a British Championship level in his spare(!) time. Oh, and he also started an independent business supplying BFS rods, reels and lures to the British Bait Finesse Community.

Web: https://www.needhamsst.com/

Photo: Jamie Needham

When and How did you first get into BFS?
I first discovered BFS around 2018 after stumbling across some videos posted by James Forrester (Perch Jesus YouTube Channel). I got really interested in the whole BFS style as it was something that looked cool, practical and fun to me. After doing a little research I purchased my first BFS Rod and reel that happened to be from Tsurinoya! It pretty much went from there and before I knew it, I had multiple set ups and was regularly importing Tsurinoya into the UK!

Photo: Jamie Needham

What got you hooked on it?
Probably the biggest thing that got me hooked had to be the downright accuracy you can achieve when casting. Before I discovered BFS I had been lure fishing with spinning reels for a couple of years, accuracy was something I really struggled with as I was using pretty unbalanced and cheap fixed spool set ups. When using a BFS set up within reason I can pretty much put my lure exactly where I want it. The ability to control the lure mid cast is a huge advantage when your regularly fishing waters with lots of cover and features. Its regularly possible to cast into exceptionally hard to reach spots by manipulating the lure mid cast, this is something which you can't really do with a fixed spool set up.

Also, not to mention how well the reels sit in your hand, I find it a damn sight easier to effectively work soft plastics and jerkbaits with a BFS set up!

Which fish species have you targeted with BFS and do you have any favourites?

I'm mainly targeting perch, chub, trout and zander (not up north though as we have none!). I do sometimes come across the rogue pike but nowadays I'm fishing to avoid them, pike are more of a blank saver if anything for me!

Probably my favourite fish to target would be perch, I know that's quite a generic answer but there's a few things that do it for me. The aggression you get on the take is something that really appeals to me, I've had some absolutely savage takes from perch and it just makes them that much better to catch.

I also love how the guys are fishing for bass in Japan, a lot of the methods we use for perch are very similar and I just love that whole BFS/Finesse style. I'd say zander come in a close second as they are just a beautiful looking fish. Trout are also something I do enjoy to target, there's nothing better than getting a hard take on a parabolic action rod while waist deep in a stream!

Photo: Harry Goodall

Tell me about Needham's Specialist tackle; when and why did you set it up - and what audience do you serve?

I started Needham's ST with the goal of making BFS, Light Casting and UL Spinning affordable and accessible to a wider audience. My journey with the business began in 2019 when I started importing Tsurinoya products, I quickly realised there was a massive market for their stuff in the UK I could use my knowledge and experience to suit their stuff to our UK style of lure fishing.

I feel like with my input lots of people have had the chance to get into BFS. It's awesome to think that people have had the chance to dip their toes into the world of BFS just by a small thing that I've done. If you looked back at the BFS Scene in the UK 4/5 years ago it was nowhere near the size it is at the moment!

This has been thanks to the input and help of multiple people in the community (including yourself Paul) to get us to where we are today. People who would not have been previously able to get into BFS now can with the access to affordable set-ups and the help and guidance of others in the community. Its something that I think is only going to get better!

What kinds of lures do you tend to fish (and what are your "confidence" options)?

Honestly, I'm really big on my creature baits. In my personal opinion these work even in water that don't have crayfish present. I think that the majority of bites you get are more because the fish (I'm talking Perch, Chub and Zander here) are interested in seeing what the lure is rather than trying to eat it.

Fish don't have hands, so there's only one way for them to see what something is and that's with their mouth. An example of this is when casting to a spot and getting hammered on the drop, I think this is 100% a reaction bite and the fish just acts out of instinct to see what your lure is.

This is even more apparent if the fish is territorial etc. as the only way for them to move it is with their mouth. At the moment I'm having great success fishing the TSU Finesse NED Worms on a Texas rig.

What was your most memorable BFS capture so far?

Nothing major but probably my 67cm PB trout from the Trent! It was absolutely hammering it down that day and to have a fish like that after fishing for 8 hours in the rain made it all worth it. Sometimes it's hard to balance fishing at the moment as I'm still working full time, running my business, racing bikes and training for my chosen sports. I'm hoping I can get my head down this coming winter and bank some really special fish!

What are your future hopes or targets for your personal BFS fishing - and for Needham's Specialist tackle?

In regards to my own fishing it would just be to have fun and meet lots of new people. I fish up and down the country and I'm always up for a new challenge. For Needham's ST I want to keep bringing new and innovative ideas to the table.

I'm sure you'll be seeing me with Tsurinoya for the foreseeable future but I'm always working on new and exciting things. At the moment there's a big gap in regards to affordable and accessible JDM Tackle here in the UK. It's just the beginning at the moment but a goal I have is to be able to supply you guys with a wide range of CDM and JDM Tackle that isn't available anywhere else.

There are some seriously innovative and unique products out there that I feel can massively benefit our style of fishing in the UK! The products we stock really speak for themselves, setting a new standard in terms of affordable and high-quality lure fishing products is something I want to continue doing for the future.

Cheers,

Jamie.

God is in the Detail

Great weather, high expectations & hard fishing

Here we go again, perfect conditions and a chance of a real mixed bag of species - where my favourite heart-breaker small stream serves up another demonic puzzle to solve. Well, they do say you're either winning or you're learning...

Arriving at the river in midsummer on a section last fished the previous winter and the small, slightly scruffy car park is almost full. There seems to be a mixture of dog-walkers, parents entertaining small kids and a few cars belonging to anglers fishing the small lake down the hill. The sun is out and the midsummer vegetation is lush and bursting out everywhere. There are quite a few fruit trees hidden in the scrubby woodland and grass fields - but not many people seem to know that. My girlfriend often has me and the kids foraging kilos of damsons and blackberries with her later in the year at this spot. The bags of fruit end up as vats of gin or jam which is totally fine by me (though we missed the wild cherries this year somehow).

As a weird contrast to this, the area round the playground itself is nearly always filled with litter and, often enough, broken glass which I see the bikers and skaters sweeping up from time to time. I've done my fair share of teenage drinking in the park growing up many, many years ago - but even then I didn't feel the need to leave crap everywhere as part of that. Sort of defeats the object of being in a park I'd have thought - but that's obviously not a view shared by everyone (though garbage does seem to annoy almost everyone in the park - young or old).

The access route to fish this section involves a smile and nod while cutting through the group of (perfectly friendly) teens smoking illicit, pungent weed under huge sycamore trees by the metal railings. The fence is easy to climb and, in dry weather, the slope down to the river is easy enough to scramble/butt-scoot down. At this time of year the air is thick with the sickly-sweet smell of Himalayan balsam (as well as the occasional ripe puffs of skunk). Arriving on a cobble beach at the bottom of a steep balsam-infested bank provides the perfect opportunity to rig up. Upstream of the beach (technically known as a point-bar; but that's the river habitat/geomorphology geek in me talking) a short riffle marked the tail end of a long glide-pool beneath a dense, tall tree canopy.

A year before this trip, I'd found some big perch in this glide (as the snapshot from then suggests) - but they seemed to move on later that year and have never returned since. Instead, today I find that there are multiple dimpling rises of small to medium-sized fish. They are eating some tiny prey items off the flat surface of the glide upstream of the shingle at the head of the riffle.

A little over a year earlier than this trip

Previous experience of that feeding style suggests either a tiny suspension or floating bait of some kind - or a small, fluttering spoon (or a fly rod of course). After failing to get a response from the first three fish I cast at with a Zoner - I switch to a little 2.5-g gold spoon with a single hook with its barb crushed down with heavy duty pliers. This is a tactic I have found to work well for surface feeding chub (which is what I now believe I am faced with). Even if the exact fish you target doesn't take the spoon, often one of its companions rushes in to grab it. The element of competition is a powerful motivator.

I get an instant take from this tactical change - yet the fish manages to shake itself free as it approaches the landing net. That bit of excitement seems to kill the pool dead with all remaining rises stopping and nothing else showing an interest in the lure. Time to move on.

Working through the next several riffles, pools and glides on a variety of soft plastics (creature/stick/swim baits) hard jerk baits plus different spoons yields absolutely no further hook-ups. However, true to form for this river, a trout that is far bigger than any I've landed from here grumpily follows a sinking minnow right the way back under the rod tip. Equally typically it refuses and turns away to slink back into the depths. It does not come back.

Given the pleasantly warm conditions and the surface-feeding activity of the chub in the first pool, there's a distinct feeling that probably the fish have experienced attention from other anglers fairly recently. This is turning out much tougher than initial expectations. I have to reverse back down the edge of this pool - as it gets too deep before you reach the riffle at its head. An awkward scramble up on to the bank, short walk upstream and then an equally-awkward slither down a nettle and bramble-covered bank lets me climb down into the water right below the riffle. The water at the spot where you can get in is a fairly deep slot at the foot of the bank - with the riffle rapidly shallowing-up as you step forwards away from the bank. That move is a bit precarious because of all the large clods of slippery clay that have eroded out of the foot of the bank. The foot of the bank is one giant slab of the stuff and it is incredibly dense - so even though it is pliable and slippery - the water struggles to erode it somehow. Getting up onto the crunchy cobble and gravel riffle away from the bank is a great relief.

Crossing the river gives access to a nice slot up against the opposite bank (to my left as I face upstream). A large, very straight, dead tree trunk lays on the river bed - almost parallel to this bank; but with its upstream end pointing a little way out into the main body of the pool. From the diameter and downward angle of the trunk (and the way it almost disappears from view the further upstream you look) it's easy to see that there is a good depth of water to this pool. If you were bass fishing, the most obvious thing in the world would be to fish baits tight up along the undercut edges of the trunk. So this is what I do now with perch in mind. I keep the spoon on for the first few casts and, when I fire one up the left side of the trunk (into the gulley between the dead tree and the overhanging vegetation from the bank) a decent size perch comes following the lure back - but I can't seem to buy a hit from these fish today.

Switching to a 38-mm Duo Ryuki Spearhead with an orange belly and a few casts later a larger perch shadows the lure back - again without committing. With that evidence of fishy interest, I spend probably 40 minutes in this pool - fishing everything from drop shot rigs with Berkley Gulp sandworms, cheb-heads and weedless floating soft stick baits, little jerk baits, sinking minnows up to 50-mm long and soft swimbaits on jig hooks. My reward? Not a single further sign of action - despite dissecting pretty much every square inch of this pool on both banks and fishing the full water column from surface to riverbed. OK, if I'd had a small buzzbait I could have given them a different topwater look - but even without that I would have expected at least a little interest.

I guess the best way to continue being skunked is to keep doing what I'm doing - so I move on to look for fresh features.

Battling my way down into a narrow, shallow run over gravel and cobbles (and flanked by low, trailing willows on both sides) I actually spot some small chub moving about around the submerged tips of the branches. I have the Duo Ryuki back on again and, second cast a smallish perch follows the bimbling progress of the little sinking minnow back to the rod tip. Two further casts and no response, I swap it for the small gold spoon and finally a fish nails it about halfway into the retrieve. Although not huge, I'm desperate for this fish to stay on long enough for a photograph.

Thankfully it does and, with the fish hovering in the water inside the submerged mesh, the shiny gold spoon reflects the jaw of the fish and the canopy of willows above. The large single hook (with crushed barb in this case) is easy to remove without a wrestling match that would remove protective slime from the fish and let electrolytes flood out of its bloodstream (and let infections invade).

Strange to think that freshwater fish are basically water-proof; otherwise their nutrients would diffuse out of their bodies and water would flood in by osmosis and kill them.

The shoal of chub is still milling about in the gap between the trailing willows so I cast again and on around the third attempt another fish nails the spoon and comes kicking into the net. The chromed cheeks and gill plates are striking.

Because these fish have come from such a tangle of branches in a tunnel of trees that is pretty difficult to access I wonder if this is a case of finding unfished water. In Japan this idea of finding, even tiny, spots that haven't been covered by other anglers is called *semenai tokuro* - or sometimes *sao nuke*. It amounts to the same thing - you're more likely to catch a fish that hasn't been harassed by multiple baits, flies or clumsy casts. It means you have to be inventive, see details that others miss or just be prepared to access (or cast into) spots where other folks can't get.

The various forms of chub and related fish around the world often have a bit of a reputation as second class citizens. I've certainly been guilty of this from time to time while targeting other fish. Possibly this comes from their terrible eating properties - but that is a bit strange when it comes to catch and release fishing. Perhaps, next to a trout, their fighting style is less flashy and slower-paced - but again a big chub is very good at digging and charging into tangled roots and branches. Whatever the reason, it is good to be reminded of how challenging and fickle they can be when targeted on lures. Yet, when the bite is on, how rewarding a method it can be particularly with BFS gear and a requirement for accurate, soft-landing casts around cover habitat. I guess this is another example of how Bait Finesse approaches can really add to the appreciation of fishing opportunities that we might otherwise miss out on.

A handful of nearly identical fish from the shoal come to the net before the rest of them get tired of the game and decline to chase the lure any longer. It certainly injects interest and fun into a really challenging session.

Almost to prove a point about under-appreciating chub at your peril (and the value of taking a moment to look closely and enjoy the fish we catch). Here is another photo of the previous fish - but with a greater focus on detail. How lucky I felt to be able to admire those patterns up close for a few seconds - it is not a view afforded to non-anglers.

To be able to spend time flicking those flat BFS casts with a tiny but dense spoon and winkle out a few fish like this was incredibly satisfying. I was a little sad to move on from this almost secret and undisturbed haven but I felt the fish had earned the right to continue with their business in private. In the next riffle above, in really fast water, I catch a tiny brown trout from a pocket behind a submerged rock - but I don't feel the need to photograph it. Instead I admire it briefly and let it swim out of the net.

Despite working diligently upstream, hopping from likely (and difficult) spot to spot I don't catch much else on this session. I find I am completely content to continue exploring and occasionally swapping out my lure. Today it is enough to have solved one small part of the puzzle and to have been forced to slow down and take in the details of the stream and the fish that have been caught. The weather is lovely and splashing about in the stream, climbing in and out of the water under the trees is just a form of happiness today.

There is a bonus blast of adrenaline as a huge green, mottled flank swoops on the lure from beneath more trailing branches. I will never know if it was a rogue pike (rare to non-existent in this stretch) or a really big perch but it just adds to the mystery and exciting possibilities of not being able to predict what the next cast will bring on this stream.

Hauling up on a ladder of thick tree-roots out of the final pool I fish I am bone-tired and completely happy. I slop my way back onto the path where the normal people are and smile to myself at what they're missing.

A rising chub photo-bombs this flat pool on my home river

Alan Ang: Fishing & Conservation Ambassador - Creator of the Bait Finesse Style Fishing Facebook Group

https://www.facebook.com/groups/BFS.fishing

Singaporean-born with a childhood spent in Malaysia & Singapore, Alan Ang is an accomplished angler, persuasive campaigner and also the man behind probably the biggest, international online community dedicated to BFS anglers "BFS (Bait Finesse Style) Fishing" on Facebook

Photo: Alan Ang

Online angling communities and the exchange of ideas they promote have been an important inspiration and resource for Alan. Then, in December 2015, he created a dedicated space on Facebook for fans of BFS which has grown quite significantly since that time to serve an audience of over 9500 members across more than 100 countries. However, the love of fishing has been part of his life since long before the dawn of the world wide web.

Alan began fishing at age five - using chunks of prawn from his grandmother's freezer as bait. With a professional fisherman for an uncle, Alan already knew plenty about which species lived in his local creek, which ones were best for eating and also how to rig, coil and store hooks and line in tin cans - ready for use.

To the likely envy of pretty much every angler I can think of, Alan's first fishing trip at such a young age resulted in amazing success. Not many people can try their hand at fishing at age five and land a catfish (as well as several large river prawns too). Now, some people I know who get to catch a fish first time out quickly lose interest because the whole game seems too easy. For Alan it seems that experience has fuelled a life-long enthusiasm for angling.

Of course, there are the familiar tales of any fishing-mad teen dashing out to fish after school. Perhaps more unconventional was Alan successfully weaving fishing trips in between duties during his stint in the Navy. It seems, though, that ultralight baitcasting lit a particular fire for him - especially after catching his first Hampala barb (Sebarau) under the guidance of a fishing friend (Halik) after meeting on an online fishing forum.

Sebarau Photo: Alan Ang

That theme of developing relationships through the opportunities offered by online communities is a recurring one for Alan. During a work trip to the UK, for instance, he has been taken fishing by Jason Vorster (who then became equally infected by the BFS bug) where the pair caught large reservoir pike and big perch. Proving how valuable the international language of fishing is, the pair got on like a house on fire and Alan quickly translated his predator fishing

Alan & Jason's UK BFS Adventure

Pike on 2-lb line while casting at perch Photo: Alan Ang

experience to success with the UK native species. During their mini-adventure, Alan recalls seeing a pod of big perch herding baitfish into a jetty before smashing them in a shower of loose scales from below as a particular highlight.

Another core, enduring theme is Alan's voluntary work to secure a bright future for fishing. His efforts in both sustainable fisheries conservation and campaigning to create mechanisms to enjoy sport fishing in Singapore are big parts of that endeavour.

Although Singapore's origins are as a fishing village - current government restrictions mean that a very small proportion of potential freshwater venues is available for recreational fishing. Heavy fines and strict regulation via CCTV enforce those restrictions. In response to this, Alan has created multiple campaigns to showcase the amazing sport fishing potential in Singapore. This has involved corresponding closely with government ministers, creating the social media movement #licensedtofishsg and collaboration with a series of like-minded groups and projects such as the Gamefish & Aquatic Rehabilitation Society and as an official representative of the International Game Fish Association (IGFA). Most anglers will recognise IGFA as the authoritative keepers of world record captures - and their mission statement broadens that out to the following quote:

"*The IGFA is a nonprofit organization committed to the conservation of game fish and the promotion of responsible, ethical angling practices, through science, education, rule making, record keeping and recognition of outstanding accomplishments in the field of angling.*"

Warm-Wading BFS for Peacock Bass Photo: Alan Ang

There can be few people who manage to successfully juggle such a large volume of voluntary work in the service of recreational angling and fisheries conservation, being the "father" of the BFS (Bait Finesse Style) Fishing Facebook Group online family and the extremely demanding professional work in his international career in the AI and big data arena.

Certainly the BFS community is extremely fortunate that Alan's passion for ultralight baitcasting has enabled him to create and foster so many relationships within our dedicated tribe. It is a wonder that, on top of all the amazing things he does for the international angling community, he still manages to post photographic trip reports of his own angling successes. Alan also does a fantastic job in reporting and maintaining what BFS is to a wide variety of anglers around the world - while qualifying that spinning rigs are their own excellent finesse lure fishing discipline.

A testament to that is the opening statement on the Facebook group which specifically welcomes trip reports from all forms of angling - with warnings of dire consequences for those who wish to denigrate those other styles of fishing. At the same time, recognising that there are some unique and valuable things that make BFS its own thing within that wider tapestry of angling styles.

Thank you Alan for all the tireless work you put in on behalf of the BFS and wider recreational fishing communities and I hope to see the success of your future iterations of #licensedtofishsg officially adopted in Singapore.

Rod Tour

Another key factor that determines your bait finesse experience is, of course, the rod. Just like the situation with BFS reels we now have access to a great selection at the full range of price-points.

Again we can enjoy the lack of barrier to entry - as well as being able to indulge in some fantastic top of the range options when budgets allow. With that said, there is no one single best rod-action or specification.

As well as varying in the obvious ways such as length or recommended lure-weight that a rod can cast, there are technique-specific and personal preferences in rod-action (bend-profile) and recovery (how quickly the rod straightens and damps out vibrations after being flexed).

Here is a quick, personal tour (necessarily incomplete - but hopefully a useful snapshot of the vast array of options out there).

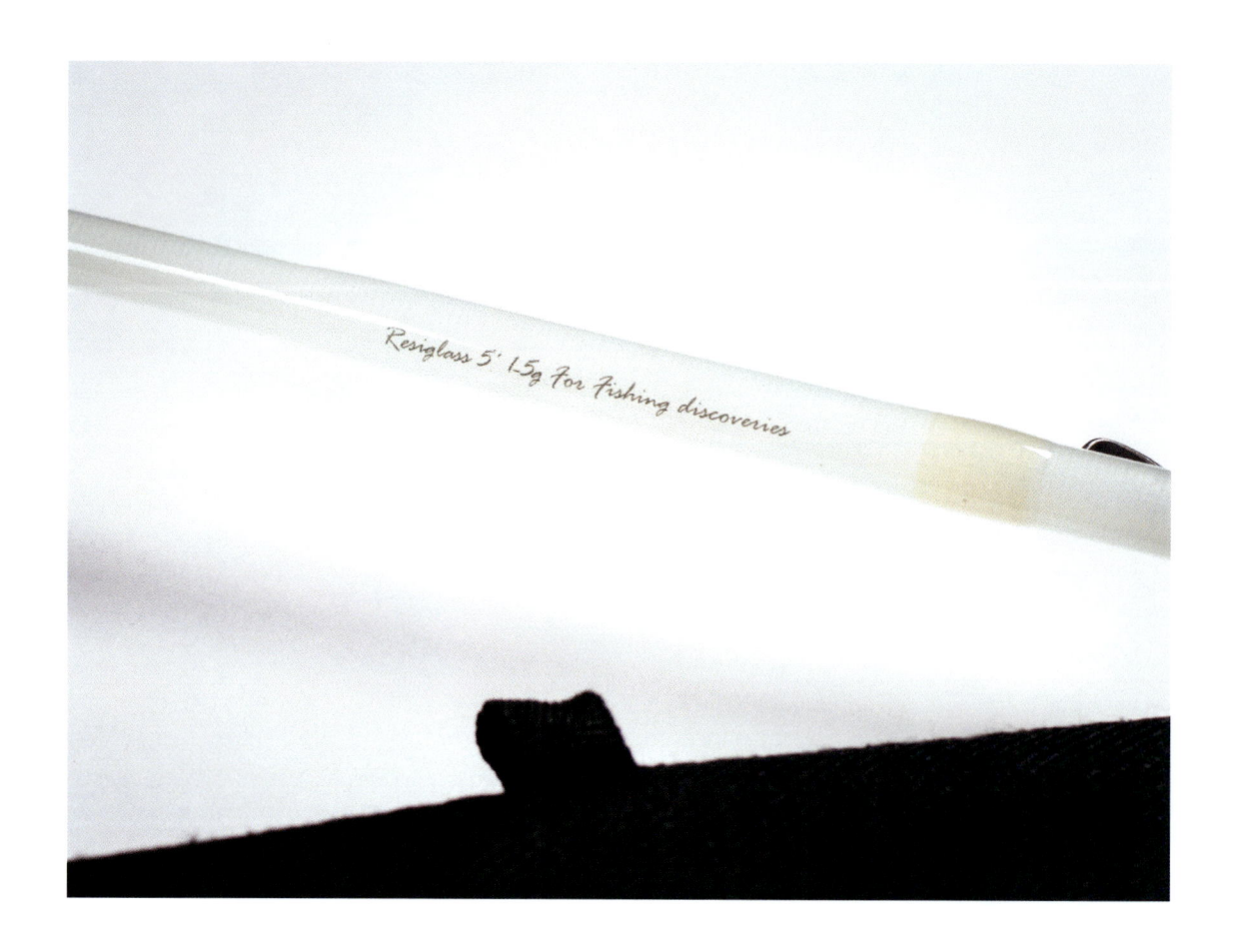

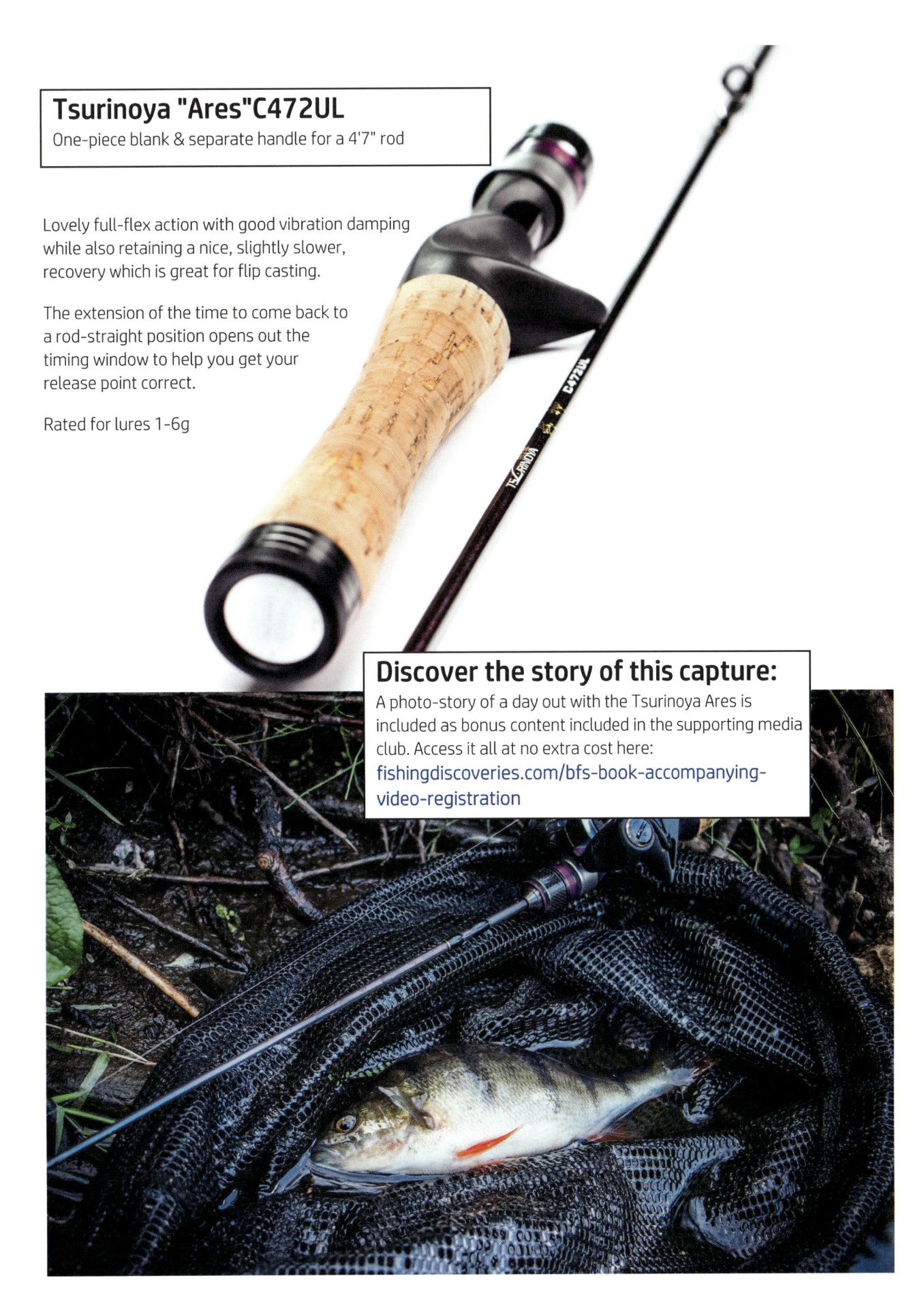

Tsurinoya "Ares" C472UL
One-piece blank & separate handle for a 4'7" rod

Lovely full-flex action with good vibration damping while also retaining a nice, slightly slower, recovery which is great for flip casting.

The extension of the time to come back to a rod-straight position opens out the timing window to help you get your release point correct.

Rated for lures 1-6g

Discover the story of this capture:
A photo-story of a day out with the Tsurinoya Ares is included as bonus content included in the supporting media club. Access it all at no extra cost here:

fishingdiscoveries.com/bfs-book-accompanying-video-registration

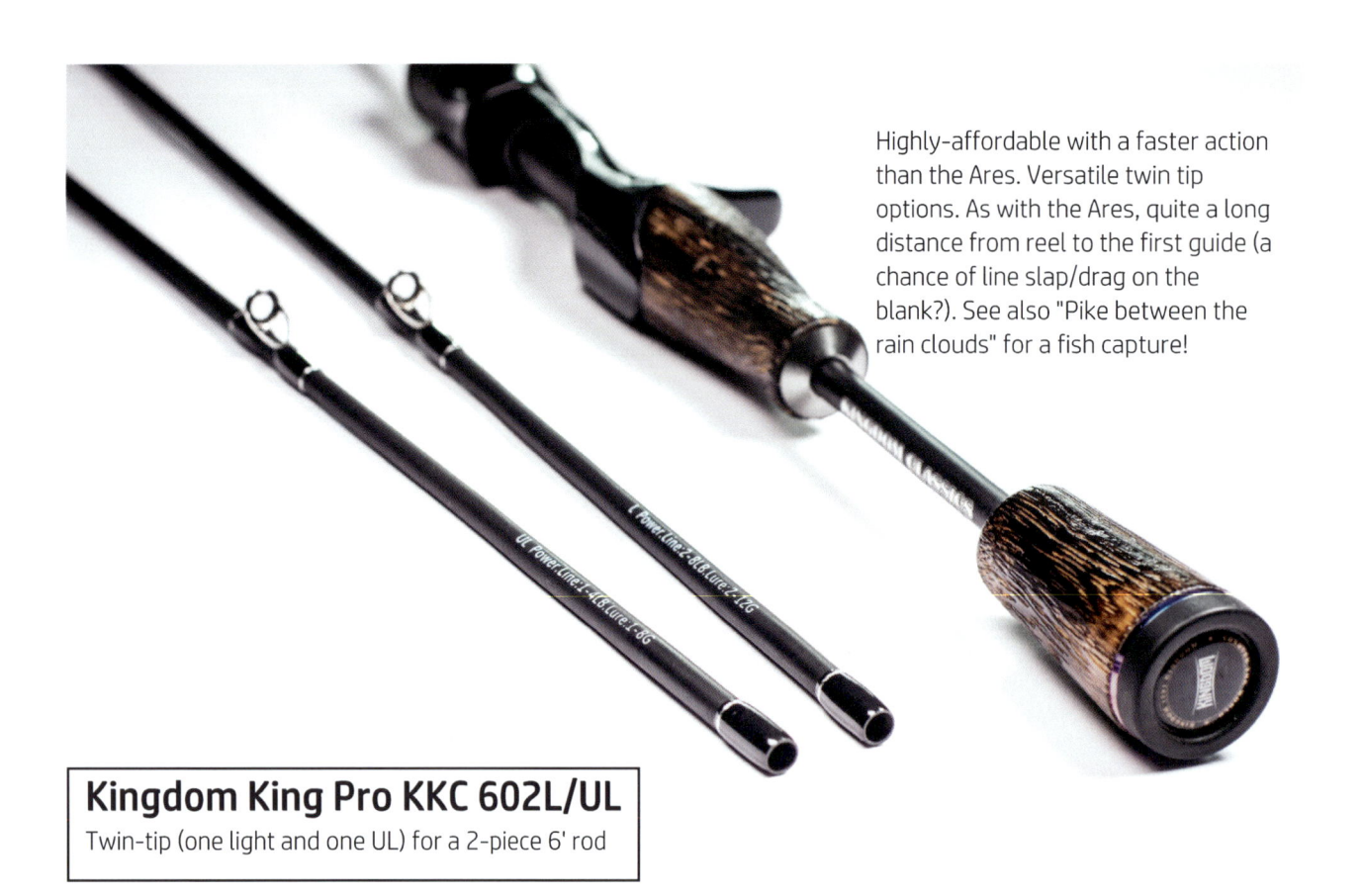

Highly-affordable with a faster action than the Ares. Versatile twin tip options. As with the Ares, quite a long distance from reel to the first guide (a chance of line slap/drag on the blank?). See also "Pike between the rain clouds" for a fish capture!

Kingdom King Pro KKC 602L/UL
Twin-tip (one light and one UL) for a 2-piece 6' rod

Ace Hawk CU Double C562UL
Two-piece blank (single tip in this version) for 5'6" rod

Another highly affordable option two-piece rod. This is the shorter (single tip) version of the 6' twin-tip CU Double. Again, relatively fast action (certainly compared to the Ares). Rated for lures 0.5-4g.

Resilure Custom S-Glass
Three-piece rod with full pour resin handle 5' rod

Darren Keats of Resilure creates some fantastic custom rods including this one in the FD Colours. The relatively fast/middle to tip action has the forgiving recovery of S-glass and is rated for 1-5-g lures. This blank is ideal for those slow motion flip casts while keeping power in reserve for subduing good-sized trout in running water.

Kuying Teton TTC 510-S
Two-piece super-ultralight BFS rod 5'10"

Kuying's "Teton" rods are a mid-priced range with extremely high build-quality. This example is their super-ultralight offering - rated for lures weighing just 0.3 - 3g (though this rating also applies to the spinning-rod version, since getting a baitcasting reel to cast a 0.3g-lure is quite a stretch!). The use of Toray carbon, un-ground/non-polished blanks (leaving nowhere for imperfections to hide) and utilising a variety of carbon-wrapping options for the (super-flexible) tip and mid/butt sections is impressive.

What can be slightly surprising about this rod is the combination of that incredibly lightweight lure-rating with the notably "fast" action. The super-flexible, hair-thin, tip quickly transitions into the stiffer sections of the blank. However, as shown in the photos, that blank is still only pencil-wide where it sits between the split handles of the rod.

While this rod is made for lures under three grams, the idea of using radically-fast action blanks is a great place to transition to some of the more specialised, stiff/fast rods. These are designed to throw relatively heavy sinking-minnow baits in fast streams (in the style showcased by Tsurinan at the beginning of this book). A strong elastic power is required for these rods to do their job with an efficient, quick flick style of casting.

Smith Multiyouse TMRK-C463L
Three-piece "sinking minnow" style BFS rod 4'6"

Rods that I'd say answer this description would include Tenryu Rayz Spectra RZS51LL-BC, the Smith TMRK-C463L (pictured in use **above** and **below** with a 5-g sinking minnow), Jackson Trout Unlimited TUSC-432L, Major Craft Finetail FSX-562L among plenty of other models.

The key qualities are the increased stiffness and crisp, faster action with that strong elastic force that won't fold-up and collapse when whipping a 5 or 7-g bait flat across the water. That relative stiffness (after all we are still talking finesse rods here) helps with picking up the sensation of the hit and also a good hook-set in those turbulent, relatively-deep trout streams.

Shimano Cardiff Native Special B42UL-3
Three-piece versatile, medium to medium-fast BFS rod 4'3"

John Pearson's first BFS rod is a really great trout stream rod to have as an introduction to that style of fishing. It is obviously highly portable (packing down to just around 17" or a nudge over 43cm). The medium to medium-fast action provides accurate, efficient casting and good hook-set capabilities.

Although it is happy to throw the sub 2-g Zoner 50SP minnows, it also copes well with baits in the 4 to 5-g range too. Being such a short rod, it works great for flip casting and feels a bit more forgiving of your timing compared to the faster "sinking minnow specialist" rods we just covered.

Rod Tour Round-up

Clearly, the key in all this is to match the length, action and overall stiffness to the baits you're fishing, the environments you're fishing in and the species you hope to catch. For lake fishing from the shore, you probably want to look at slightly longer rods. Not only do they tend to give you extra casting distance, they also help to reach out over marginal vegetation and obstructions. In those situations flip casting (which favours a shorter rod) won't tend to figure as commonly as it would while wading a small stream

Alternatively, throwing 7 to 10-g topwater baits for hard-fighting peacock bass, takes a rod with some more backbone. Kevin Mai's trip reports later in the book share his choice for that role.

You'll also need to keep in mind the need to match the spool-weight and braking capabilities of your reel to both the rod-action and lure-weight. While this isn't intended to be a deep-dive instructional book, just be aware that casting a stiffer rod with some force could really get that spool spinning fast at the start of your cast!

I hope the pictures and rapid-fire tour of some examples of rods and their characteristics might just provide some inspiration...

Acehawk CU Double C562 UL & Alphas Air TW 20

John Pearson: Bait Finesse Convert Tackles the "Why Not Just Use a Spinning Reel?" Question

I have to admit to being something of a sceptic when my fishing partner Paul first started disappearing down the BFS rabbit hole. My first thoughts were something along the lines of "what could this gear offer that I can't already do with my ultra-light lure/spinning gear?"

That sentiment is something I see cropping up again and again in the online fishing community - and on the one hand, if you're happy with your UL spinning setup that's all good, but (as I found out over time) you're missing out in a big way if you completely overlook what BFS has to offer.

The real revelation was not so much in the fishing side by side UL vs BFS as, in these situations, we both had our fair share of fish... no, the real revelation was what I was able to see when filming and (probably more importantly) editing the footage I'd shot of Paul fishing with BFS gear.

I think getting behind a camera and then editing the footage gives insight and perspective you just don't get from spending time watching in person. Being able to replay moments again and again, to freeze the action or slow it right down let's you observe subtleties few people ever get the chance to.

I know this phenomenon played a huge part in my development as a fly angler where I spent ten years filming the six times English national fly fishing champion (John Tyzack). Being able to film and playback every moment of a truly elite angler's approach is a privilege few people ever get but the subtleties were not only a revelation to me but sometimes to JT himself and this made me realise what a valuable tool filming and watching such footage can be.

When Paul and I first started fishing and filming together we were discovering tenkara during its emergence outside of Japan. Routinely filming each other on stream provided us valuable insights into our techniques and their successes and shortcomings. This (coupled with the transferable skills of several years' experience with long rod/long leader fly fishing) enabled both of us to progress very rapidly in our tenkara skills eventually travelling to Japan many times and gaining praise and endorsement from several of Japan's tenkara masters.

I'm not just digressing into this territory to say "ooh look at me, I filmed a national champion and went to Japan"... there's a MASSIVE advantage to be had from the feedback video footage of yourself and people of higher skill levels than you. Being able to compare yourself in a third person perspective offers huge insights if you're looking to improve your skills.

Almost everyone has the capacity to do this now with modern smart phones offering fantastic video capability and many with amazing slow motion too. If you can find a buddy to pair up with on stream, I can't stress enough how valuable it can be to spend some time filming one another's technique (there's probably room here for a shameless plug of our own video tuition media to help you with this too).

So what was the big revelation I got when filming BFS???

The single big advantage that shone through on camera time and again was the massive difference in the flight path and velocity of lures cast with BFS over the same lures cast using a spinning reel. This was something that's much more noticeable with slow motion footage too.

A lure cast from a fixed spool/spinning reel outfit has a fairly constant velocity as it travels to its target and (even with great "feathering" and line control) the lure lands with a comparatively heavy "splash" for its given mass.

Comparing this with the same lures cast from a well tuned BFS outfit (especially in slow motion) it's very noticeable how the velocity of the lure is gradually slowed by the reel's brakes as it reaches its target. This means the splash for any lure's given weight is much reduced. When fishing on shallow rivers for spooky fish (which is what we do a lot) the advantage of a more delicate landing of the lure is clear.

We often need to land the lure really close to complex cover such as undercut banks or overhanging vegetation where fish are lying to get the fish to follow our lure but a heavy splash can easily spook the fish. In these scenarios BFS wins every time.

There's also the marginal advantage of that tight contact from rod tip to lure maintained by the braking effect of a baitcaster versus the more unpredictable contact achievable with a spinning reel and also the slightly faster "pickup" when you start winding as opposed to the "lag" of closing a bail-arm.

I've had more than a decade of experience fishing a baitcaster with jerkbaits for pike (the Shimano Curado Bantam CU 201) so baitcasters weren't completely alien to me but I'd always joked that the only way Paul would get me switching from spinning reels and UL lure to BFS was if I had a round reel (I'd taken a liking to the Shimano Calcutta Conquest BFS) and a super short fibreglass rod (I have Angler Saito videos to thank for that fetish!)

With the data stacking up from extensive filming and editing it became impossible for me to remain objectively sceptical of the advantages I was seeing and the jokes about round reels and fibreglass rods turned into the reality of the pictures you'll see in this section and the video media accompanying this book. Not to mention the money pit of JDM hardbaits that I just HAD to get to go with my setup.

The actual on stream techniques are not really any different whether you choose UL spinning gear or BFS but I'm absolutely convinced the latter offers a few key advantages, especially where the fish are spooky... but it's not just about the cold science and statistics, there's a much improved "feel" for me with a nicely tuned reel and a fibreglass rod that I never had with my spinning reels and whether real or imagined I'm certainly happy to call myself a BFS convert!

Peacock Bass in Singapore with Kevin Mai

Kevin does an amazing job of sharing his inspiring trip reports with members of the BFS (Bait Finesse Style) Fishing Facebook group. He has kindly allowed me to use a selection of his trips and photos here so that you can get a feel for this high-octane approach to targeting the hard fighting Peacock Bass (or Brazilian tucunaré). Native to South America, there are many species of these large predators belonging to the cichlid family. In Singapore, two species are said to have been introduced, Cichla orinocensis (Orinoco Peacock Bass) and Cichla temensis (Slender Peacock Bass) according to ecologyasia.com

Photo: Kevin Mai

February 21st 2021

Saturday turned out to be another super productive session out in the water again! My buddy brought the heavy gear and I stuck to BFS. We waded to a cove full of clear water as far as the eye could see with little grassy patches here and there. Shortly after we began, I'm already hooked on. But the fishes kept getting off the hook. On the 4th hookup, I finally managed to land a fish; first catch of the day with the spybait! As we walked on, I decided to try a finesse swimbait, but only got one very ambitious Goby. Dark clouds were coming in, so we decided not to go in as deep as we initially planned and headed back to the cove where the fishing was still good. Back out comes the spybait, and almost immediately hooked on and landed one more decent size Peacock Bass. On BFS setup, they fight hard like nothing else, but on such a clear cove with no structures, I had time and patience on my side. My buddy was also catching good fishes as he had the range and power for advantage. He switched to a wakebait and targeted the grassy weeds by the far end bank. After a few cranks the water exploded and it was another fish on for him! As he reeled it in closer, I could see 4-5 more Peacock Basses swimming alongside his. One quick and excited cast, and I was also hooked on for a double! By far, the most exciting part of our session!

Superb day of fishing, with multiple catches between the two of us!

Rod: Rapala Classic Countdown travel rod

Reel: Shimano Calcutta Conquest BFS HG

Line: Berkley Fireline Crystal 4lb + Varivas Light Game Ti-F shock leader 8lb

Lure: Duo Realis Spinbait 62 Alpha, Duo Spearhead Ryuki Quattro 70s

Photos: Kevin Mai

August 5th 2021

What started out as a slow day became an incredibly productive session! Day began slow with me being the only one in the group whose yet to catch a fish. The fish seemed to be going after jerkbaits at the moment, so I switched out for a suspending jerkbait of my own. A slow constant retrieve with a few light twitches ,and it was fish on! Landed two juvenile peacocks to get the ball rolling. We waded out to a deeper water area and came across a sunken tree along the bank. Fish love to nest there. It was the perfect opportunity to test out my new floating swimbait lure. I casted it out on towards the edge of the tree branches and worked it along the edge with a constant twitch to give it that "left-right" cadence. With no warning, there was just a soft "bloop!" and my lure disappeared into the water. Fish on! I tightened the drag just a little bit more so to bring it away from the branches for a safe landing. First decent sized fish on the day with very vibrant colours, totally engulfed the lure! Things got slow again after that. I switched out to the reliable spybait again. Once again it failed to disappoint and I was rewarded with another beautiful 3lb peacock with three solid bars.

One of the group broke his personal best with a 4.5lb peacock. After helping him land it and snap a few pics. I went on to cast off. No sooner did he released his fish I got another peacock hooked on. Another good size 4.5lb peacock on the spybait! What a shame there couldn't be a double catch shot. Very enjoyable session with multiple catches to go around!

Rod: Rapala Classic Countdown travel rod

Reel: Shimano Calcutta Conquest BFS HG

Line: Sufix 131 G-Core 4lb + Sunline Small Game Leader FCII 8lb

Lure: OSP Asura Durga 73sp, Biovex Joint Bait 72sf, Duo Realis Spinbait Alpha 62

Photos: Kevin Mai

Photos: Kevin Mai

August 26th 2021

The morning started with us wading into clear calm waters. Immediately we spotted a pair of peacocks within casting distance. Topwater didn't catch their attention. Neither did jerkbaits.

I decided to switch out to a soft plastic on a jighead and see if I could piss off the male by dangling it about its face. After a while, I felt a strong pull and it was fish on! Not the male, but the female came in for a nice snapshot. Still a decent sized fish with a solid hookup! Switched locations and saw more spawning pairs along the bank. I switched to a sinking minnow and the bites start rolling in. A frenzy started right within casting distance and we got a double hookup! A very enjoyable session.

Rod: Rapala Classic Countdown travel rod

Reel: Shimano Calcutta Conquest BFS HG

Line: Berkley Fireline Crystal 4lb + Varivas Light Game Ti-F shock leader 8lb

Lure: Island Anglers Grumpy Grub + VMC Coastal X Jighead, Duo Spearhead Ryuki 50s

Farewell Fishing Trip with Duncan...
A Swedish Send-off in Yorkshire
Insta: @duncanphilpott

Duncan is one of the smartest people I know. Mathematician, mountain-biker, pro-photographer and now GIS tech-innovator and river restoration analyst. He started fishing after a photography gig to cover world-class pro mountain bike racing took him to New Zealand and he came across fly fishing (as you do). Despite being a relative newcomer I'd say he's already better than at least 90% of fly fishers will ever be. Duncan is also someone who I don't get to fish with half as often as I would like to (because of work schedules).

So, when he told me he had landed a job in Sweden and needed to box all his stuff up in Yorkshire, I figured we should probably fish together the very next chance we got. Since Duncan likes his UL spinning as well as the fly and tenkara rods, I reckoned a trip targeting perch and trout would be a great way to share a late-summer day using BFS and UL Spinning on a river we both know well for fly fishing (but was new territory on the lure).

I have to admit, online maps are pretty fantastic. The specific section of river I had in mind was not one Duncan had fished before - though he had fished extensively either side of it. This spot was close to one of the (several) houses I lived in here over the years before I moved away to another town - and I knew a semi-secret access route. However, to describe the appropriate parking spot and how to defeat the one-way system in words would be nearly impossible. *Praise be to the digital map-pin* is all I can say.

We converge on the spot from opposite points on the compass and, judging by progress with donning waders he hasn't beaten me here by an embarrassing margin. I still apologise anyway - since three tries out of four I arrive after Duncan for these things. Here, among the terraced housing, it is difficult to be inconspicuous while climbing into chest waders - so the best plan is to tackle it boldly and look like you do this sort of thing every day. In fact, when I used to live in the area, that wasn't too far wide of the mark - so the performance is at least somewhat authentic. After shrugging on the braces, taking out the rod and shouldering the sling-pack a quick look around gives us the green light to slip between the garages and down the steep, loose slope to the river.

Part way down there is a small, level section of path and it is wise to retrieve the reel from the pack and attach to the rod here (rather than opening everything up over the water while standing knee-deep). The nice thing about these short trout-stream rods is that they are really easy to handle and thread beneath even a pretty tight canopy. Today I want to fish a glass rod with the Ambassadeur - while Duncan opts for his trusty UL spinning set-up. We start out dropping speculative casts here and there as we walk downstream to see what's what. One of the nice things about fishing with people on your wavelength is that you can leap frog each other with easy familiarity - and you want them to succeed *almost* as much as your own ambition to enjoy that special catch.

We each call out things that we notice - signs of a fish, where to watch your step in between easy chat about recent puzzles and successes on other trips. Reaching the road bridge it seems worth heading down under for a few exploratory casts before getting on with our main plan of forging upstream as far as time will allow us. At this early stage, the weather is living up to the forecast's word and sunlight is glinting off the ripples. With little recent rain, the water is transparent (albeit carrying the regulation tea-coloured peat-stain). Just now, the river feels a little bit sleepy - at least for the predators in it. I know that there are trout and grayling here - with the grayling probably making up the larger numbers. I think there should be some perch here too; though finding that out for sure is a major part of the challenge we've set for today.

With no fishy contact, we head back up above the bridge and Duncan kindly takes my camera to shoot a few frames with line and glass rod back-lit by the sun. The lens I have on isn't really fast enough - but the light and the chance to frame some flat casts through the leaves still creates a pleasing composition in his hands. That little 1.7-g Zoner Minnow flies out there sweetly enough too. Again no contact here - but I know this spot is much better for grayling anyway, and those guys don't so often take a jerk bait (small soft plastic creature baits are more their speed).

Time to move up again.

Hanging back to let Duncan fish through up above me I fire off a few pictures to catch the UL spinning angle for the record. At this stage he's fishing a white soft plastic swim-bait with a paddle tail and it certainly looks good in the water.

It's also really good for watching in flight against the generally dark background to this section of water (as you can see **above**). From the angle of the line coming off the reel you can also tell why the first line-guide on spinning rods sits out much further from the blank.

Aside from a couple of abortive follows in the section up to this point, neither of us has generated much action so far. However, the deeper pool just above that white water is what I had in my mind's eye as a potential perch-hole when we cooked up the idea for this trip. While I think about switching out my light Zoner for something heavier, Duncan goes all in on a Ned rig with a kind of "pin-tail floating, soft stick-bait" in a really drab/dirty olive colour and dark flake.

Now the cloud cover has come in and there is a sneaky hint of rain ahead - not sure that was in the script...

I bump two fish in quick succession at long range in a back-eddy on the light minnow (both trout by the feel of things). Meanwhile, Duncan's plastic sits up vertically just perfectly off the flat, mushroom head. Almost exactly on-cue, it takes just a few little hops across the bed of this pool before he is hooked up on something that is nodding and kicking in a distinctly non-trout-like fashion. I manage to scramble up onto the bank behind him. The water is really deep just here - even close in - and it's a good job Duncan is much taller than me. Fishing the camera out of the sling-pack I get a shot off just as the fish is netted. I'm delighted to see that it is a lovely, chunky perch. Mission accomplished and an ideal netting-shot to use at the start of this story. Kneeling on the bank to get the lens close to the water yields a suitably moody image of this stripy warrior (**opposite**) and I feel genuine gratitude to Duncan for conjuring him up.

Finally taking the hint and realising just how deep that drop-off is, I switch to a 5-g sinking minnow (Tsurinoya DW63) and immediately get hit. I swear loudly at missing the hook-up. Then on the next cast the twin of Duncan's fish follows the minnow in right to my feet and swipes viciously around - missing (or avoiding) it at the last second. However, as suddenly as that action began, it tails off. I think Duncan loses his lure on a snag - at any rate the next time I look he is fishing that swimbait jig again. In an unspoken agreement we begin working up the stonework along the opposite bank in search of the next honey-hole.

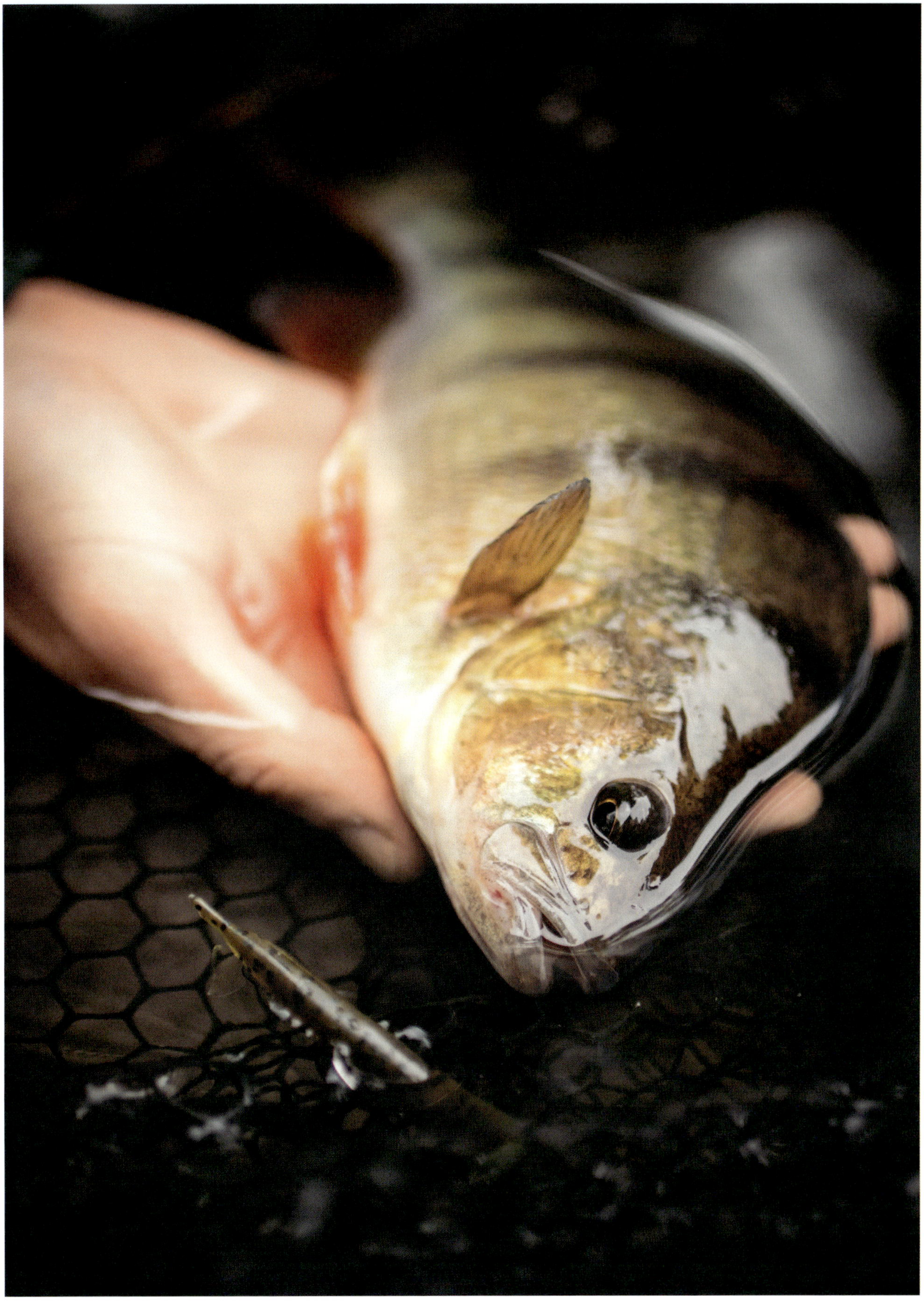

I hang back a little to watch Duncan fish for a while and we soon reach the end of that piece of stonework. The river gives way to a shallower run with scattered rocks. Again, it is a section I know well, so I'm as happy to watch as I am to participate. Interest and tail nipping from trout is getting more frequent now - unusual with a falling barometer on this river.

Just as the downpour starts I fire off a picture of Duncan upstream of me (**left**) so I can put the camera back in the waterproof sack while it is still relatively dry. That gives me a nice excuse to turn back to fishing. In this shallow, trouty, run the Zoner goes back on. A flat, backhand cast peels nicely out toward the foam-line (why is it so satisfying to watch the Abu line-guide shuttle back and forth on the cast?). When everything locks up tight to a fish it has the sensation of that really being the only possible outcome of this cast. I don't mean that my skills somehow made it all happen. Absolutely the opposite in fact.

What I mean is the way everything just seemed to line up together at that moment. With the conditions waking the trout up, a little extra life being put into the flow by rainfall (but without extra colour)- that already set things up. Then the lure dropping gently into just the sort of spot a trout would hover out into from cover as it came on the feed. I suppose this is what a flow state feels like, almost like passively observing the thing unfolding from inside my own head. Glass rod hooped over and a lively trout splashing water up at me as the rain falls down creates an odd sort of symmetry. Kneeling in the water and making the final turns with my "wrong" hand on the old right-hand-wind reel creates a short enough line that the rod can be drawn back to slide the fish into the net.

The trout (**opposite**) surprised me with its pale greyish flanks, widely-spaced, round, dark spots and pearl-grey halos round each; an unusual look for this part of the river. It is such a fine wild creature and as it rests in the water there's only time for a short burst of photos before the camera gets too wet. Looking at the rain drops beaded up on the reel while the cork is rubbed slick by handling perfectly evokes the sensation of being out in the warm, wet summer elements. As the fish kicks strongly away I feel that is enough time spent in self-absorption and hurry to catch up with Duncan to compare notes at the bridge.

We take turns flicking casts below and under the bridge, turning a few fish before climbing out to walk around a much deeper section. On the top-side of the bridge three kids and a couple of observers are set up on the bank - fishing a spot together. We exchange wishes for good luck and give them plenty of space before dropping back into the channel.

Because time feels quite short today, it doesn't take much (any) debate to decide to put the camera away and just enjoy time on the river with good company and good fishing. Sorry about that. As satisfying as capturing those memories is, it's really important to know when to just engage in the pastime and ditch the multitasking. Since this book is, for the most part, a shout out to the pure enjoyment of fishing - it seems essential to walk that walk often enough to avoid fishing ever coming to feel like "work". That's my excuse anyway - and I'm sticking to it.

We wade on up through lovely streamy water turning a great trout each. A quiet spell follows and I nearly ship water over the top of my chest waders stepping into a deep hole at the foot of someone's back garden. I laugh because Duncan has about a foot more clearance to the top of his waders - and this section is just zero problem for him. Working up along some very tasty looking stonework that has perch written all over it strangely yields nothing - yet arriving at a bend-pool with a tree growing in a curve out of a crumbling stone-wall; deep water around its roots. Comparing this to the previous stonework, is it just possible that the fish prefer this 100% perfect habitat instead? Again I get cautious follows from a pair of good perch. Hmm, those stripy guys are really playing hard to get again.

Digging out the phone to check the clock shows it really is time to turn around. Alright then, three last casts (make that five). Throwing a heavy sinking minnow up into the fast, turbulent flow (just where it joins the slow cheek of deep water) towards the head of the next run upstream a trout slams it and the forgiving glass rod keeps it pinned all the way to the net. It's beautiful in that red-spotted wild brown trout way - stunning actually. A perfect exclamation point to the fishing so that even I don't want to tarnish it by making further casts.

Reeling up and wading/scrambling back to the cars I want to say thanks to Duncan for being a great fishing buddy - but there doesn't seem to be a good "guy-way" to say it (we are in taciturn Yorkshire after all). Instead I ask him how the packing and planning is going - and wish him luck with the whole thing. I think he gets the basic sentiment.

Anyway - I get to say it here:

Thanks man, I always enjoy our trips and they are always too few.

P.

Lure Tour

As well as rhyming, a quick tour of my lure box completes the snapshots of the main hardware involved in BFS (Reel, Rod & Lure).

Once again, because this *is* just a snapshot of what I currently have in rotation, it reflects the venues and fish that I target the most. Out there in the real world, there are way more lures than anything else involved in Bait Finesse.

Suppliers like Bait Finesse Empire, Nine Seven Tungsten, Needham's Specialist Tackle and many more have an ever-growing selection of cool treats to offer your target fish.

Probably the most obvious missing style of baits here are various kinds of top-water baits (either micro buzz-baits, poppers, frogs or pencils).

Still, that gives me a good excuse to go shopping soon!

2.8-g Duo Ryuki Spearhead 38S

1.7-g Major Craft Zoner Minnow 50 SP

Rapala Ultralight Minnows 4-cm Slow Sink

Vacuma 2.5-g Spoon

Aioushi 3.5-g Spoons

5-g Tsurinoya DW63 50-mm Sinking Minnows

3-g Tungsten Cheburashka head (Nine Seven Tungsten), size 6 offset worm hook and 50-mm Korum Snapper Squirmz in motor oil/red flake

1-g Daiwa Prorex Jig hook with Fox Rage Spikey Drop-shot micro shad (hot olive colour)

3-g Tungsten Cheburashka head (Nine Seven Tungsten), size 2 offset worm hook and 65-mm Nine Seven Baby Claw ("Gary" colour)

Glow in the Dark!

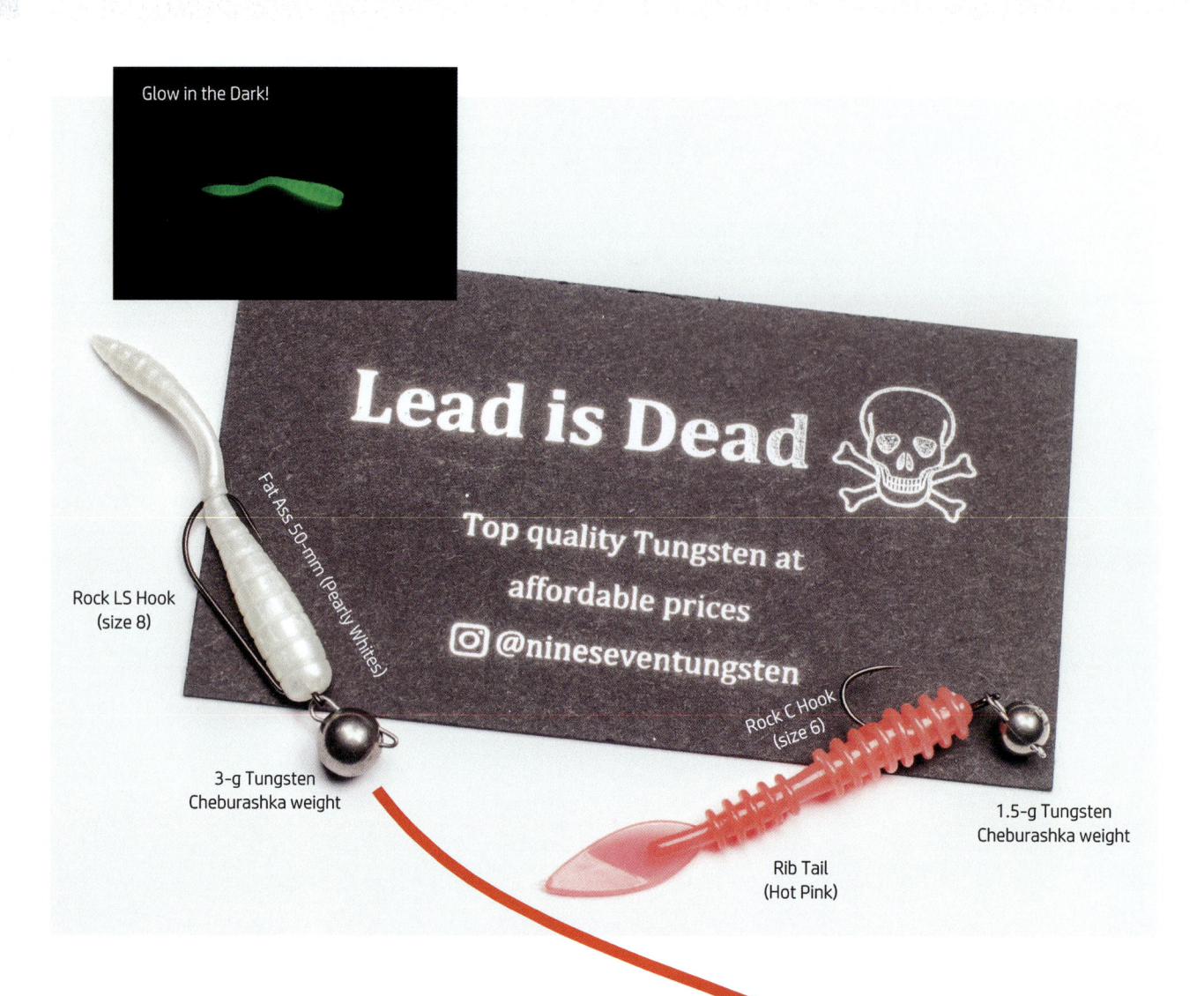

Lead is Dead

Top quality Tungsten at affordable prices

@nineseventungsten

Rock LS Hook
(size 8)

Fat Ass 50-mm (pearly whites)

3-g Tungsten
Cheburashka weight

Rock C Hook
(size 6)

Rib Tail
(Hot Pink)

1.5-g Tungsten
Cheburashka weight

144

My First Home-made Balsa Minnow

I got kind of addicted to the satisfying sensation of watching lure-making videos on YouTube. Probably it was inevitable to want to try actually making one too. If you subscribe to my BFS club emails then the story of how I created it, the first outings - some success and then the disaster of smashing it into steel sheet-piling (before a phoenix from the flames repair job) will already be familiar.

Probably the most important things to take from the process (for me at least) are the sheer pleasure and satisfaction of actually catching a fish on something you spend hours creating - plus the enhanced appreciation you get for other lures on the market. Understanding even a little more about the lure-maker's art lets you get much further under the skin of the lures you might buy from professional brands and makers.

Closing Message & Profound Thanks

So here we are at the end of this collection of thoughts, stories, insights and memories. Right now it seems that we are still very early in the process of BFS breaking out of Japan and beginning to grow around the world. As well as the timeless enjoyment of technically-satisfying fishing methods and highlighting the value of fishing friendships, I hope that this might be an interesting snapshot in time to look back on.

No doubt the development of gear will sweep onwards rapidly and some of the tackle photographed here could quickly come to look very much "of its time". Although, of course, I couldn't resist including quite a few photos of that 1977 Abu reel - so I'm sure several other designs will also stand the test of time.

I do want to thank everyone in the awesome bait finesse community - the interactions online and in person with members of this tribe seem to be unusually positive. Thank you for inspiring my own experiments and adventures with UL baitcasting. A big thanks to my partner in crime over so many projects and buddy John Pearson - and I knew you'd get hooked on this stuff too ha ha! Many thanks also to Jason Todd for "*letting me play with your tackle*" fnarr fnarr!

Naturally, I need to extend profound thanks to all of the contributors to this book - and I guess alphabetical order is the only way I can go with this. While we are all sitting around the metaphorical BFS Camp-fire, thank you so much to:

Alan Ang

Amir Azzabi

Anorak SZN

Christopher Lee Lian Li

Duncan Philpott

Hobie-Wan Kenobi

Jamie Needham

Jimmy Ly

Kevin Mai

Tsurikichi Nikke

Tsurinan

Japanese post-fishing BBQ & Beers

Finally, thank you to you also for reading this book and engaging with the project (and for being part of the global BFS community). I hope that you enjoy, not only the contents of these pages, but also the special supporting media in your "owner's membership area" online space. I look forward to your comments inside that free bonus membership course within our Fishing Discoveries Academy. Do also feel free to contact me via email with your BFS stories, suggestions and comments on:

paul@fishingdiscoveries.com

Dr Paul Gaskell

South Yorkshire, Nov 2021

Printed in Poland
by Amazon Fulfillment
Poland Sp. z o.o., Wrocław
05 December 2021

36c8b2b7-9f6a-4153-b320-75f4774c362fR01